The Mystery We Celebrate,
the Song We Sing

Kathleen Harmon, SNDdeN

The Mystery We Celebrate, the Song We Sing

A Theology of Liturgical Music

A PUEBLO BOOK

Liturgical Press   Collegeville, Minnesota
www.litpress.org

A Pueblo Book published by Liturgical Press

Cover design by David Manahan, OSB. Cover illustration: *Cantoria*, sculpture detail, by Luca della Robbia, 1431–1438. Museo dell'Opera del Duomo, Florence, Italy.

Library of Congress Cataloging-in-Publication Data

Harmon, Kathleen A., 1944–
    The mystery we celebrate, the song we sing : a theology of liturgical music / Kathleen Harmon.
        p.   cm.
    "A Pueblo book."
    Includes index.
    ISBN 978-0-8146-6190-1
    1. Music—Religious aspects—Catholic Church.   2. Church music—Catholic Church.   I. Title.

ML3921.4.C38H37 2008
264'.2—dc22   2007049975

Contents

Introduction

Throughout the years of my professional ministry as a liturgical theo-logian and musician my primary interest has been to explore *why* the church always sings the liturgy. The singing is not accidental or arbitrary, but a necessary and integral part of the ritual.[1] Liturgical documents, scholarly investigations, and pastoral writings on liturgi-cal music generally take this connection between liturgy and music for granted; few have offered any theoretical explanation for this rela-tionship.[2] Aidan Kavanaugh has put it this way: "Music is the mode . . . by which the liturgical act gets done."[3] But what, specifically, is the liturgical act that is being done, and why is music the mode of its doing? How is it that music conveys the liturgical mystery to the people who are celebrating it? What exactly is the mystery being con-veyed? And what is the essential connection between this mystery and the music the assembly is singing?

Answering these questions meant pursuing theological investiga-tion into the liturgy itself. *Sacrosanctum Concilium* provided my start-ing point by stating that in her liturgy the church comes together to celebrate the paschal mystery.[4] My project became clear: I needed to

---

1. Vatican II, *Sacrosanctum Concilium*, *Acta Apostolicae Sedis* 65 (1964): 97–134; English trans. taken from *Vatican Council II: The Conciliar and Post Conciliar Documents*, ed. Austin Flannery, OP, new rev. ed. (Northport, NY: Costello Publishing Company, 1992), no. 112; hereafter referred to as *SC*.

2. Two scholarly works that have addressed the question of why music is so intrinsically related to liturgy are Edward Foley's "Toward a Sound Theol-ogy" in *Ritual Music: An Introduction to Liturgical Musicology*, ed. Edward Foley (Beltsville, MD: Pastoral Press, 1995), 107–26; and Judith Kubicki's *Liturgical Music as Ritual Symbol: A Case Study of Jacques Berthier's Taizé Music* (Leuven, Belgium: Peeters, 1999).

3. Aidan Kavanaugh, "Beyond Words and Concepts to the Survival of Mrs. Murphy," in *Music in Catholic Worship: The NPM Commentary*, ed. Virgil Funk (Washington, D.C.: Pastoral Press, 1983), 99.

4. *SC*, no. 6.

show how liturgical singing participated in and facilitated ritual enactment of the paschal mystery.

I began with the paschal mystery itself and found the answers I sought in the theological work of Joyce Ann Zimmerman, CPPS,[5] who defined the paschal mystery as a dialectic tension between the "not yet" (soteriology) and the "already" (eschatology) of human redemption and liturgy as ritual enactment of that dialectic. Musically, this meant that singing, which is integral and necessary to liturgy, must in some way catalyze and facilitate ritual enactment of this dialectic. But how? What gives music, and particularly singing, the power to do this? I needed to identify those properties of music that gave it the capacity to participate in and facilitate enactment of the paschal mystery. Here

5. Joyce Ann Zimmerman, CPPS, "Liturgical Catechesis and Formation in Light of the *Constitution on the Sacred Liturgy*" in *Singing Faith into Practice: Essays in Honor of Robert W. Hovda, Series II* (Silver Spring, MD: NPM Publications, 2005), 15–27; "Eucharist: Renewing Worship, Renewing Life" in *Year of the Eucharist: October, 2004–October, 2005*, Essays by the Faculty of the Athenaeum of Ohio (Cincinnati: Athenaeum of Ohio, 2005), 41–45; "Eucharistic Adoration and *Missio*," *Liturgical Ministry* 13 (Spring 2004): 88–95; reprinted in *National Bulletin on Liturgy* 37/179 (Winter 2004): 236–45; "Beauty and the Beast: Criteria for Artful Liturgy" in *Postmodern Worship & the Arts*, *Festschrift* in honor of James L. Empereur, SJ, ed. Michael E. Moynahan, SJ, and Douglas Adams (San Jose, CA: Resource Publications, Inc., 2002), 21–32; "Eucharist and Justice" in *A Book of Readings on the Eucharist* (Washington, D.C.: NCCB Secretariat for the Third Millennium and the Jubilee Year 2000, 2000), 71–78; "Paschal Mystery—Whose Mystery?: A Post-Critical Methodological Reinterpretation" in *Primary Sources of Liturgical Theology: A Reader*, ed. Dwight W. Vogel (Collegeville, MN: Liturgical Press, 2000), 302–12; "Liturgy Notes," *Liturgical Ministry* 8 (Spring 1999): 102–8; "A Theology of Liturgical Assembly: Saints, Relics and Rites," *Liturgy* 14:3 (1998): 45–59; "Liturgical Assembly: Who Is the Subject of Liturgy?" *Liturgical Ministry* 3 (Spring 1994): 41–51; *Liturgy as Living Faith: A Liturgical Spirituality* (Scranton: University of Scranton Press, London and Toronto: Associated University Presses, 1993); "Language and Human Experience" in *New Dictionary of Sacramental Worship*, ed. Peter Fink (Collegeville, MN: Liturgical Press, 1990), 644–51; *Liturgy as Language of Faith: A Liturgical Methodology in the Mode of Paul Ricoeur's Textual Hermeneutics* (Lanham, New York, London: University Press of America, 1988).

I found the work of Walter J. Ong, SJ,[6] Victor Zuckerkandl,[7] and David Burrows[8] invaluable. Ong illustrated how sound reveals presence, binds hidden interiorities, and manifests power. Zuckerkandl demonstrated how music reveals the true nature of reality and facilitates our participation in the being-ness of the world. He showed further how music reveals time to be a generative force of existence, a notion that indicated that music shared liturgy's manner of reckoning time. Burrows presented a schema of three fields of human action and described the differential operation of sound, voice, and music within each of these fields. He defined sound and voice as an interaction between force and resistance and articulated how this force-resistance interaction plays itself out in the three fields of human action vis-à-vis a changing center-periphery relationship between self and other. Burrows argued that music functions as entryway into the third field of human action where barriers between center and periphery collapse in an experience of the self's oneness with the whole of reality. The work of these scholars paved the way for me to say that communal singing is necessary to liturgy because it facilitates personal communion and does so through a force-resistance dialectic that parallels the soteriological-eschatological dialectic of the paschal mystery.

STRUCTURE OF THE BOOK

Chapter 1 presents the theological and liturgical foundations for saying that liturgy is ritual enactment of the paschal mystery. The chapter begins with a summary of Paul's understanding of the mystery of Christ, and moves from there to a describe the paschal mystery as a dialectic between the "not yet" (soteriology) and the "already" (eschatology) of human redemption. The chapter next examines the term enactment, defining it as ritual remembering whereby a community reenters its founding events in an ongoing and generative

6. Walter J. Ong, SJ, *The Presence of the Word: Some Prolegomena for Cultural and Religious History* (New Haven and London: Yale University Press, 1967); *Orality and Literacy: The Technologizing of the Word* (London: Methuen, 1982; rpt., London and New York: Routledge, 1988).

7. Victor Zuckerkandl, *Sound and Symbol: Music and the External World*, trans. Willard R. Trask (New York: Pantheon Books, 1956; Princeton: Princeton/Bollingen 1969; 1973); *Man the Musician: Sound and Symbol*, vol. 2, trans. Norbert Guterman (Princeton University Press, 1973; Princeton/Bollingen, 1976).

8. David Burrows, *Sound, Speech and Music* (Amherst: University of Massachusetts Press, 1990).

way. The chapter then shows how liturgy mediates past and future existence through present action. Finally, the chapter analyzes the surface structure of the eucharistic rite in order to disclose the rite's deep paschal mystery structure as well as a dynamic of presence that catalyzes this disclosure.

Chapter 2 presents the musical explorations that enable us to say that music—and specifically liturgical singing—participates in an essential way in liturgical enactment of the paschal mystery. The chapter explores the relationship between music and personal presence, between music and participation in being, between music and the experience of time, and between music and the force-resistance tension embedded in human relationships.

Chapter 3 establishes correlations between the theological and liturgical foundations of chapter 1 and the musical investigations of chapter 2. This chapter shows how liturgical singing is an integral mode by which the Christian community encounters and appropriates the paschal mystery because it (1) enables the assembled community to become present to God, to themselves, to one another, and to the liturgical action in which they are engaging; (2) opens them to the deepest level of participation in being, that of their identity as Body of Christ; (3) immerses them in time as a transforming force of Christian existence; and (4) works out within and among them the soteriological-eschatological dialectic of the paschal mystery through the force-resistance dialectic of sound and song.

Chapter 4 identifies some pastoral implications and challenges flowing from a theology of liturgical singing as enactment of the paschal mystery. This chapter extrapolates beyond the more narrow scope of the three preceding chapters and demonstrates practical and pastoral applications of the theology I have developed.

PARAMETERS OF THE BOOK

Common speech often uses the terms "liturgy" and "worship" interchangeably in reference to public prayer events within organized religions. In this book I distinguish between the terms, using "liturgy" to refer to normative patterns of public prayer that have a codified, formal, repetitive structure, and "worship" to refer to liturgy as well as to forms of uncodified, unstructured, and nonrepetitive public prayer. Within these parameters, "worship" includes private, individualized devotional acts, whereas "liturgy" encompasses only acts of worship that are public and communal. Liturgy is communal worship formally structured along ritual patterns laid down by the norms of a given worshiping tradition. Its form, although open to adaptation and development, is not arbitrary, but fixed; it "preexists" the local community that enacts it. The liturgical ritual I explore here is that defined by postconciliar Catholic understanding and practice.

Numerous terms such as church music, sacred music, liturgical music, ritual music, and so forth, have been and are used to denote music used in Christian worship. Because of its denotation as music integral to the reformed liturgy of Vatican II, I use the term "liturgical music." Furthermore, I focus on vocal music, and principally on music sung by the assembly rather than by cantor or choir. For Catholics liturgical music is primarily vocal and is directed toward enhancement of the words to which it is united. The music under consideration here, then, is communal singing that *is* the rite, that is, sung elements through which the assembly enacts the rite by singing it (for example, the acclamations sung during the eucharistic prayer); and communal singing that *undergirds* the rite in a significant way, that is, sung elements that support the rite's underlying movement toward personal presence and intentional participation (for example, the hymns or songs that accompany the entrance and Communion processions of the eucharistic liturgy).

I do not pursue a comprehensive investigation of the nature of music (no study can); rather, I explore aspects of music that explain its integral connection with liturgy's enactment of the paschal mystery. I examine aspects of the nature of sound, of voice and word, and of music and song from a generalized perspective rather than from the more specific angle of the liturgical functions of certain forms of music or musical elements. Because of the limited scope of this book, I do not address the sociology of music, or specific ethnomusicologies, or even the psychology of music. Nor do I pursue the science of acoustics (although I do explore the nature of sound), or the philosophy of music (although I do touch upon philosophical issues). Rather, I explore phenomenological elements of sound, voice, music, and song that support my conviction that communal singing is integral to liturgy because it enables the assembly to participate in ritual enactment of the paschal mystery.

Because my aim is to articulate a theology of liturgical music in terms of music's relationship to ritual enactment of the paschal mystery, this book is not concerned with specific ritual elements within the liturgy (for example, the entrance procession or the gospel acclamation), but with the entire rite as a single action. Nor is it concerned with the specific functions of music within the rite (for example, the purpose and placement of processions and the subsequent function of music in relation to these processions), but with the deep structure that engenders music's integral relationship with the rite as a whole. Rather than examining the surface structures of the liturgical rite, I explore its deep structure—the paschal mystery being enacted beneath and through the surface structures. In terms of liturgical music, my intent is to pursue how it is that this "not-at-hand" depth structure is encountered through the "at-hand," embodied phenomenon of communal liturgical singing. Hence, I explore the integral relationship between music and liturgy through a methodology of theological speculation rather than functional analysis.

In 2004 Liturgical Press published *The Ministry of Music: Singing the Paschal Mystery*[9] as part of its reedited and expanded Collegeville Ministry Series. That book was a practical, pastoral implementation of a theology of liturgical music based on living and celebrating the paschal mystery of Christ. *The Ministry of Music* outlined only briefly, however, the theological core that lay at its heart: that there is an intimate relationship between the paschal mystery we celebrate in liturgy and the music we sing for this celebration. This present book offers a deeper look at a theology of liturgy as enactment of the paschal mystery and the role music plays in that enactment. This book is intended for liturgical music scholars, graduate students, music directors, and anyone seeking a deeper theological understanding of the role of music within the liturgy. Its content is geared toward an audience prepared to grapple with the theology, philosophy, and musicology it presents. In the final chapter I identify pastoral implications and challenges this study generates, but those seeking more thorough pastoral application of the theology presented here are directed to other related writings, in particular *The Ministry of Music: Singing the Paschal*

9. Kathleen Harmon, *The Ministry of Music: Singing the Paschal Mystery*; Collegeville Ministry Series (Collegeville, MN: Liturgical Press, 2004).

Mystery; *The Ministry of Cantors;*[10] and my Music Notes column in *Liturgical Ministry*.

ACKNOWLEDGMENTS

This book is a revision and summary of my doctoral dissertation. I am grateful to Dr. Robin A. Leaver of Drew University, who guided my research and who shared with me his enthusiasm for the music of the church and its role in the church's worship. I will be forever grateful for his generous gifts of time, expertise, and encouragement.

I wish also to thank my religious congregation, the Sisters of Notre Dame de Namur, who have supported me in the pursuit of both music and scholarly study and who continue to call me to the fullness of liturgical living. I wish to express gratitude to my family and especially to my parents who first nurtured me in Christian living and liturgy and who continue to model its meaning in daily life. I am grateful to Peter Dwyer of Liturgical Press who refused to let this material sit on my shelf but insisted I get it translated into readable form and out to the public. I am appreciative of the time Robert Zimmerman donated, as a nonmusician and nonliturgist but as an educated person in the pew, to a careful reading and commentary on this material.

Finally, I wish to thank Joyce Ann Zimmerman, CPPS, friend and colleague, who graciously assisted me in editing this work for publication, and who in both scholarship and Christian living continually shows forth what it means to embrace the depths of the paschal mystery.

10. Kathleen Harmon, The Ministry of Cantors, Collegeville Ministry Series (Collegeville, MN: Liturgical Press, 2004).

Chapter 1

Understanding the Paschal Mystery

Since Vatican II the term paschal mystery has become paradigmatic for understanding the meaning of Christian life and identity.[1] It was through the paschal mystery that Christ achieved his mission of redeeming humanity and giving glory to God. It is the paschal mystery into which all members of the church are immersed through baptism. It is the paschal mystery that marks the mission of the church, the Body of Christ grafted onto Christ through baptism into his death and resurrection.[2]

The paschal mystery can be defined as the mystery of the Cross, an image that emphasizes the self-giving death of Christ as the means of our salvation. The paschal mystery can also be described as a *transitus*, emphasizing Christ's experience of "crossing-over" from death to resurrection and correlating with the passing-over of the Israelites from the slavery of Egypt to the freedom of the Promised Land.[3] A third way of describing the paschal mystery, and the way we will use here, is as the dialectic tension we experience between the "already" of redemption completed in Christ and the "not yet" of salvation still being worked out within and among us. This description opens a way for us to see the paschal mystery not only as the experience of Christ but also

---

1. Jeffery Kemper, "Liturgy Notes," *Liturgical Ministry* 8 (Winter 1999): 46. *Sacrosanctum Concilium* uses the phrase paschal mystery eight times: nos. 5 (twice), 6, 61, 104, 106, 107, 109. The *Catechism of the Catholic Church* structures its entire presentation on liturgy around the notion of paschal mystery (see Part II, and especially nos. 1067, 1068, 1085, 1104, 1164, 1165, 1362–64).

2. Vatican II, *Sacrosanctum Concilium, Acta Apostolicae Sedis* 65 (1964): 97–134; English trans. taken from *Vatican Council II: The Conciliar and Post Conciliar Documents*, ed. Austin Flannery, OP, new rev. ed. (Northport, NY: Costello Publishing Company, 1992) no. 6; hereafter referred to as *SC*.

3. See Irmgard Pahl, "The Paschal Mystery in Its Central Meaning for the Shape of Christian Liturgy," *Studia Liturgica* 26:1 (1996): 19–20; hereafter referred to as "The Paschal Mystery in its Central Meaning." Also, Patrick Regan, OSB, "Paschal Vigil: Passion and Passage," *Worship* 79:2 (2005).

as the defining pattern of *our own* identity and living. The tension between the "not yet" and the "already" of salvation marks daily Christian experience; it also defines the deep structure of Christian liturgy.

PASCHAL MYSTERY IN THE TEACHINGS OF PAUL

The notion of paschal mystery is derived primarily from the Pauline tradition. St. Paul uses the term mystery (Gk. = *mystérion*) to refer to the plan of God conceived before creation for the salvation of the world (Eph 1:3-10; 3:9-11; Rom 8:2-30) and fully realized in the life and person of Jesus Christ (2 Cor 1:20) through whom all things are reconciled to God (Col 1:13-20; Rom 5:9-11).[4] For Paul there exists only one mystery, the mystery of Christ, and Paul feels compelled to lead all peoples to grasp this plan hidden for all eternity in God (Eph 3:9-11).[5]

Despite his certainty about the decisiveness of the Christ event for salvation, Paul remains acutely aware, however, of an incompleteness about human salvation. Humankind still struggles to be saved (1 Thess 5:9; 1 Cor 3:3; 10:12-13). Built into the human condition is the "not yet-ness" of *our* 'unfinished business' in completely conforming ourselves to Christ."[6] The fullness of time has already arrived in the life, death, and resurrection of Christ. God's salvific plan is already fulfilled (Gal 4:5); the "new creation" is already present (2 Cor 5:17); "the end of the ages" has already come (1 Cor 10:11) because Christ has

4. See Günther Bornkamm, "*mystérion*" in *Theological Dictionary of the New Testament*, ed. Gerhard Kittel, trans. and ed. Geoffrey W. Bromiley (Grand Rapids, MI: Eerdmans Publishing Company, 1967) 4:802–28; Joyce Ann Zimmerman, "Liturgy Notes," *Liturgical Ministry* 8 (Spring 1999): 102–8, for a summary of the Pauline concept and its use in the mystagogical writings of Cyril of Jerusalem, Ambrose of Milan, Theodore of Mopsuestia, and John Chrysostom; William G. Thompson and Joyce Ann Zimmerman, CPPS, "Mystery" in *The Collegeville Pastoral Dictionary of Biblical Theology*, ed. Carroll Stuhlmueller (Collegeville, MN: Liturgical Press, 1996), 657–61; and Joseph A. Fitzmeyer, SJ, "Pauline Theology" in *The New Jerome Biblical Commentary*, ed. Raymond E. Brown, Joseph A. Fitzmeyer and Roland F. Murphy (Englewood Cliffs, NJ: Prentice-Hall, 1990), 1382–1416. For examples of *mystérion* in the Pauline and Deutero-Pauline writings, cf. 1 Cor 2:1-2, 7; 4:1; 13:2; 14:2; 15:51; Rom 11:25; 16:25; Eph 1:9; 3:3, 4, 9; 5:32; 6:19; Col 1:26, 27; 2:2; 4:3; 2 Thess 2:7.

5. This and all subsequent citations are from NRSV.

6. Zimmerman, *Liturgy as Living Faith: A Liturgical Spirituality* (Scranton: University of Scranton Press, London and Toronto: Associated University Presses, 1993), n. 49, 157; italics original.

definitively overcome sin and death. Yet we still live in a world struggling for salvation, marked by sin, and cursed by death. This living both in the "not yet" (soteriology) and in the "already" (eschatology) of redemption is distinctive to Pauline eschatology.[7]

Paul clearly perceived the "not yet"–"already" tension built into the process of human salvation. He also perceived the intimate connection between the mystery of Christ and the community of those who have been baptized into Christ. For Paul, baptism radically transforms our identity. Baptism immerses us in the death and resurrection of Christ (Rom 6:3-5), transforms us into being the Body of Christ (1 Cor 12:12-13, 27), and missions us to collaborate with Christ in bringing God's salvific plan to fulfillment (Col 1:24-25). For Paul, God's hidden plan of salvation revealed and fulfilled in Christ requires our collaboration. Salvation is not a single act (i.e., Jesus' death on the cross) but an ongoing process whereby we must cooperate with God to bring the divine plan of salvation to completion not only for ourselves but for the whole world.[8] We have a part to play in the plan.

The paschal mystery, then, includes the entire saving mystery of Christ—his life, mission, passion, death, resurrection, ascension, sending of the Spirit, and promised return at the end of time—and *our* participation in that mystery. The paschal mystery is not only a past event related to the historical Christ; it is also a present event unfolding in our lives today and in the life of the church as a whole. We have a part to play in the plan.

7. For discussion of biblical and systematic notions of soteriology and eschatology see A. Yarbro Collins, "Eschatology and Apocalypticism" in *The New Jerome Biblical Commentary*, ed. Raymond E. Brown, Joseph A. Fitzmeyer, and Roland F. Murphy (Englewood Cliffs, NJ: Prentice-Hall, 1990), 1359–364; Dermot A. Lane, "Eschatology" in *The New Dictionary of Theology*, ed. Joseph A. Komonchak, Mary Collins, and Dermot A. Lane (Collegeville, MN: Liturgical Press, 1990), 329–42; John J. Collins, Carolyn Osiek, and Zachary Hayes, "Eschatology" in *The Collegeville Pastoral Dictionary of Biblical Theology*, 261–68; Dianne Bergant, Mary Ann Getty, and Robert J. Schreiter, "Salvation" in *The Collegeville Pastoral Dictionary of Biblical Theology*, 867–71; Francis Schüssler Fiorenza, "Redemption" in *The New Dictionary of Theology*, 836–51.

8. Getty, "Salvation" in *The Collegeville Pastoral Dictionary of Biblical Theology*, 870: "Salvation is a process to be finally realized rather than a single act. Although this process is initiated by God, it requires cooperation with God's grace, as Paul warns the Philippians: 'work out your salvation with fear and trembling.'"

PASCHAL MYSTERY AS DIALECTIC TENSION OF CHRISTIAN LIVING

The term dialectic can refer to the tension or opposition between two interacting forces or elements. It can mean a process of argument in which opposing ideas are pitted against one another to arrive at truth. Hegel applied the term to the process of change in which an idea or concept is subsumed and fulfilled by its opposite. Following a different tack, French philosopher Paul Ricoeur develops the notion of dialectic as an ongoing tensive interplay in which neither pole ever disappears or becomes subsumed by the other; rather, both poles remain ever present, and it is their ongoing tension that generates new understanding, new meaning, and new ways of being.

Ricoeur's dialectic approach forms our basis here for describing the paschal mystery as a dialectic of soteriology and eschatology.[9] The tension between redemption already completed and salvation not yet

9. I am indebted to Joyce Ann Zimmerman, CPPS, for this notion. Conceiving of the paschal mystery as a dialectic tension between soteriology and eschatology is the seminal insight driving all her theological work and writings. See her "Liturgical Catechesis and Formation in Light of the *Constitution on the Sacred Liturgy*" in *Singing Faith into Practice: Essays in Honor of Robert W. Hovda, Series II* (Silver Spring, MD: NPM Publications, 2005), 15–27; "Eucharist: Renewing Worship, Renewing Life" in *Year of the Eucharist: October, 2004–October, 2005*, Essays by the Faculty of the Athenaeum of Ohio (Cincinnati: Athenaeum of Ohio, 2005), 41–45; "Eucharistic Adoration and *Missio*," *Liturgical Ministry* 13 (Spring 2004): 88–95; reprinted in *National Bulletin on Liturgy* 37/179 (Winter 2004): 236–45; "Beauty and the Beast: Criteria for Artful Liturgy" in *Postmodern Worship & the Arts, Festschrift* in honor of James L. Empereur, SJ, ed. Michael E. Moynahan, SJ, and Douglas Adams (San Jose, CA: Resource Publications, Inc., 2002), 21–32; "Eucharist and Justice" in *A Book of Readings on the Eucharist* (Washington, D.C.: NCCB Secretariat for the Third Millennium and the Jubilee Year 2000, 2000), 71–78; "Paschal Mystery—Whose Mystery?: A Post-Critical Methodological Reinterpretation" in *Primary Sources of Liturgical Theology: A Reader*, ed. Dwight W. Vogel (Collegeville, MN: Liturgical Press, 2000), 302–12; "Liturgy Notes," *Liturgical Ministry* 8 (Spring 1999): 102–8; "A Theology of Liturgical Assembly: Saints, Relics and Rites," *Liturgy* 14:3 (1998): 45–59; "Liturgical Assembly: Who Is the Subject of Liturgy?" *Liturgical Ministry* 3 (Spring 1994): 41–51; *Liturgy as Living Faith: A Liturgical Spirituality* (Scranton: University of Scranton Press, London and Toronto: Associated University Presses, 1993); "Language and Human Experience" in *New Dictionary of Sacramental Worship*, ed. Peter Fink (Collegeville, MN: Liturgical Press, 1990), 644–51; *Liturgy as Language of Faith: A Liturgical Methodology in the Mode*

come constitutes the very core of the paschal mystery; it both explains how this mystery can belong to Christ and to us and describes how we experience this mystery in our lives. The reality of resurrection (the eschatological fulfillment of redemption) does not erase the reality of death (the soteriological state in which we find ourselves); rather, the two stand as ongoing polar opposites in the process of Christian living and transformation. Their dialectic tension can be articulated as numerous polar opposites—as not yet-already, soteriology-eschatology, this world-the next, death-resurrection, and so forth.

The paschal mystery that characterizes Christian living and Christian liturgy is an *ongoing tensive interplay* between death and resurrection, sin and redemption, fidelity and infidelity. We experience this polar tension in multiple ways in daily life. At some points (often when least expected) the resurrection side of the mystery dominates our experience as, for example, when peace negotiations between warring nations or tribes arrive at some settlement, or reconciliation occurs between a disaffected parent and offspring. At other points (and this perhaps most of the time) the dying side of the mystery overwhelms us as we struggle; for example, through the prolonged illness of a terminally ill spouse, or as we watch on the evening news the report of yet another terrorist bombing of innocent people and feel powerless before the overwhelming presence of so much evil in the world. But at no point in our living does either pole ever cancel out the presence of the other. Both remain, and it is their *creative tension* that generates our movement forward in discipleship and fidelity. Struggling with tensions such as sin-reconciliation, unity-disunity, justice-injustice, etc., forces us to grapple with our identity as Body of Christ and allows the self-emptying of the paschal mystery to become progressively more formative of our self-understanding and behavior.

PASCHAL MYSTERY AS DEEP STRUCTURE OF CHRISTIAN LITURGY

One of the principal contributions of *Sacrosanctum Concilium* was recovery of the early church understanding of liturgy as the privileged enactment of the paschal mystery. The mystery of God's saving action reached its climax in the death and resurrection of Christ. The liturgy enables us to enter and participate personally in this mystery, not by

---

of Paul Ricoeur's Textual Hermeneutics (Lanham, New York, London: University Press of America, 1988).

applying past merits earned by Christ, but by actually making the saving events of Christ present here and now. Four avenues of exploration can help us understand how liturgy is able to do this: (1) the notion of enactment, (2) the concept of time, (3) a hermeneutics of liturgical enactment, and (4) an analysis of some liturgical rites.

Notion of Enactment[10]

Enactment as ritual remembering. Enactment is a form of ritual remembering in which the meaning and power of a past event become actualized in the present. There is a substantive difference between this kind of remembering and the remembering of reminiscing or storytelling. The latter is simple retelling or dramatization; enactment, on the other hand, is *anamnesis* (Greek; Hebrew root: *zkr*), a form of remembering through ritual celebration by which a people actualize the power of their founding events in the present and for the future:

> [A]namnesis is the simultaneous evocation of the past, present, and future dimensions of human reality. Those who "make memorial"—especially with others in the context of religious ritual like the Passover—not only call the past into the present, but in doing so are affected by that past in such a way that their future is also changed.[11]

In dramatization or reenactment the past that is retold, regardless of its importance for those engaged in the retelling, remains in time past. Every year on Christmas Day, for example, residents of Washington's Crossing, Delaware, act out George Washington's wintry transport of troops across the frozen Delaware River on December 25, 1776.

10. I use the term "enactment" rather than "reenactment" because the latter is sometimes applied in a way that defines liturgy as only dramatic re-presentation of past events (as in, for example, Eucharist as "reenactment" of the Last Supper). Liturgy, however, is always more than "reenactment"; it is *actualization* of past events in present and future temporalities.

11. Mark R. Francis, CSV, "Remembrance, Pastoral-Liturgical Tradition" in *The Collegeville Pastoral Dictionary of Biblical Theology*, 825. See also Pahl, "The Paschal Mystery in Its Central Meaning," 20: "Through making remembrance, which the people in the case of both instituting actions [i.e., Passover and Eucharist] are commanded and empowered to do (Ex. 12:14; Lk. 22:19; I Cor. 11:24, 25), God opens up the possibility for the people again and again to make themselves present to the unique saving event to which they owe their existence and from which they draw the strength to live, and thus to become partakers in that event's abiding effect."

Although the original happening has importance for Americans, it is nonetheless an event that is external to those reenacting it. They are not Washington and his troops. One factor that attests to this exteriority is the attention paid to historic costumes, boats, and other artifacts in the reenactment: the authenticity of the dramatization is evaluated in direct proportion to the realism of these artifacts. The actors must clothe themselves with historical garb (in other words, hide their true identities) for the ceremony to seem real. This very attention to historic detail indicates that the ceremony is a reproduction or representation of a past event that, outside of this reproduction, no longer exists. Such dramatization is not ritual enactment but simple representation, its meaning and staging every year as limited by a discrete and transitory moment in time as the original event it represents.

The distinction between enactment and dramatization can be further clarified by examining the referents of each. We can act in or observe the reproduction of Washington's crossing of the Delaware and be reminded of the heroic greatness of one of the founders of the United States of America. We can reflect on the sufferings of those revolutionaries who struggled through this nation's founding war. But these reflections remain about persons and events no longer present and demand no action on our part in response. The remembering does not necessarily catalyze transformation of values and behaviors on the part of those doing the remembering. By contrast, the referents of *anamnesis* include not only the founding person or event being remembered, but also the present enactors, for enactment has as much to do with their being and identity as it does with that of the founding person or event. Ritual enactment leads a people to encounter anew who they are and who they are meant to be and in so doing invites them to choose new ways of being that deepen their identity.

Enactment as entry into originary events. Not every event from the past can be enacted; enactment happens only in relation to events that are originary to a people, that bear enduring paradigmatic meaning, and that carry eschatological significance.

The term "originary" bears a different nuance from the word "original" and is not be confused with it. "Original" implies that an event is once-and-only, time bound, and finished. "Originary" implies that an event continues through time and affects ongoing identity.[12] Originary

12. Cf. Zimmerman, note 3 on p. 78 in *Liturgy as Language of Faith*.

events can be defined as those historic happenings, actions, and/or persons bearing three significant levels of import. First, such events are inaugural, that is, they set into motion the beginnings of a people.[13] They are looked upon as the person(s) and/or event(s) that brought a people into existence and determined their sense of identity. Thus, the Exodus event inaugurated the Israelites as God's chosen people, and the Christ event inaugurated the church as Body of Christ.

Second, these persons or events are seen as paradigmatic for all time. They shape the pattern of daily existence and of behavioral choices and they determine the face of the future. Thus, the Israelites understood that they must be faithful to the covenant living to which their identity as God's people called them and that the God who had saved them from Egypt would always act on their behalf at decisive future moments. Thus, the Christian community believes that because of the Christ event the outcome of self-sacrificing death will always be resurrection, and that the pattern of faithful Christian living is the on-going challenge to surrender to this mystery of death and resurrection.

Third, these persons or events carry eschatological import, that is, they bear upon the ultimacy of time and meaning.[14] Originating in the past, they disclose in the present the shape of the future. For Israel, Moses and the Exodus event set history on a definitive course for which a salvific future was guaranteed. For the church, the Christ event stands in the same light: both historical and transhistorical, the paschal mystery of Christ pushes all creation forward to its assured redemption in the plan of God.[15]

Because originary events inaugurate identity and mission, because they are paradigmatic for all time, and because they bear eschatological import, they are not restricted by chronological time boundaries—that is, by the separation of time into past, present, and future—but remain perennially present and active. Once-and-for-all events that

---

13. What Theresa F. Koernke refers to as "the charter event which has brought the group into existence" in "An Ethics of Liturgical Behavior," *Worship* 66 (January 1992): 27. See also Pahl, "The Paschal Mystery in Its Central Meaning," 20.

14. Alexandre Ganoczy, *An Introduction to Catholic Sacramental Theology*, trans. William Thomas (New York/Ramsey: Paulist Press, 1984), 109.

15. *Catechism of the Catholic Church*, no. 1085.

give meaning to the past, the present, and the future are continually existent and bear defining force on the meaning of existence.[16]

Enactment as generative. Through ritual enactment a community enters its originary events in an ever fresh, generative way.[17] Ritual enactment makes the events active in the present and determinative of the future because it enables the community to enter and experience its defining origins in a way that recommits the community to specific action born out of that identity. The originary events remain ongoing and operative because enactment continually reconstitutes the identity and mission that the events catapulted into history. Thus enactment is ritual activity that has to do with the ongoing presence and power of events originary to a people's identity and mission and has to do with transformation of life, that is, with the appropriation of new ways of living prompted by the new self-understanding derived from the ritual confrontation with and recognition of identity. Enactment generates the future by transforming current self-understanding and consequent behavior.

Liturgy as Christian ritual enactment. The preeminent means whereby the Christian community enacts its originary events is the liturgy.[18] Liturgy is the privileged activity whereby the church

16. Ganoczy, *An Introduction to Catholic Sacramental Theology*, 109. Alexander Gerken states it thus, "The ultimate remains," *Theologie der Eucharistie* (Munich: Kösel, 1973), 57; quoted in Ganoczy, *An Introduction to Catholic Sacramental Theology*, 109. See also *Catechism of the Catholic Church*, no. 1165: "When the Church celebrates the mystery of Christ, there is a word that marks her prayer: 'Today!'—a word echoing the prayer her Lord taught her and the call of the Holy Spirit. This 'today' of the living God which man [*sic*] is called to enter is 'the hour' of Jesus' Passover, which reaches across and underlies all history."

17. See Walter Brueggemann, *The Message of the Psalms: A Theological Commentary* (Minneapolis: Augsburg, 1984), n. 10, 197: "In psalm study, the crucial work of Mowinckel suggests that in the cult something genuinely new was wrought. That is, the cult is not mere replication, but is a generative action."

18. See for example, *SC*, no. 2: "For it is through the liturgy, especially in the divine Eucharistic Sacrifice, that "the work of our redemption is exercised. The liturgy is thus the outstanding means by which the faithful can express in their lives, and manifest to others, the mystery of Christ and the real nature of the true Church," (see also nos. 5, 6, 61, 102); *Eucharisticum mysterium* (*Acta Apostolicae Sedis* 59 [1967]): no. 25: "Whenever the community gathers to celebrate the Eucharist, it announces the death and resurrection of the Lord, in the hope of his glorious coming"; *The Milwaukee Symposia: A Ten-Year Report* (Washington, D.C.: National Pastoral Musicians Association and Chicago: Liturgy

encounters and celebrates the paschal mystery as her mystery and chooses ongoing surrender to its call. In and through the liturgy the church enacts the death and resurrection of Christ as a present, ongoing event. This death and resurrection is not external to the community celebrating it, but is the very substance of their Christian living. We need not bring external artifacts of costume and makeup to the enactment; we need bring only ourselves and our lives as they are for the enactment is, in fact, a celebration of our identity. We are not observers at a memorial dramatization but participants in an enactment of self-understanding and self-actualization. The portrayal of the crossing of the Delaware is a celebration of Washington's life, Washington's struggles, Washington's victories. By contrast, liturgical enactment of the paschal mystery is celebration of our life and identity as Body of Christ. What we engage in when we celebrate liturgy is not reproduction or representation or dramatization, but *anamnesis*.

As enactment of identity, liturgy is an ontological moment: it has to do with being and identity. But liturgical enactment is also an existential moment in that the remembering involved—*zkr*—is always directed toward subsequent action:[19] It has to do with how we choose to live. The enactment actualizes a tradition of laws and values and engages our recommitment to these. In the case of Christian liturgy, what is actualized is God's covenant with humankind established in Christ and mediated through the church. Participation in liturgy renews this covenant and transforms our living according to the values inherent in this covenant. In the case of the annual celebration of Washington's crossing of the Delaware, the ceremony demands no action, either of

---

Training Publications), no. 28: "All liturgical preparation begins in simple recognition of one event at the heart of every liturgy: the paschal mystery"; Louis-Marie Chauvet, *Symbol and Sacrament: A Sacramental Reinterpretation of Christian Existence*, trans. Patrick Madigan, SJ, and Madeleine Beaumont (Collegeville, MN: Liturgical Press, 1995), 477: "[O]ne cannot understand the anamnesis *except by starting from the 'paschal mystery'* of Christ, and not from anything anterior to it" (italics original); Zimmerman, *Liturgy as Living Faith*, 89: "[L]iturgy is a privileged manifestation of the Paschal Mystery, a door to our own self-understanding"; Pahl, "The Paschal Mystery in Its Central Meaning," 37–38: "[T]he liturgy brings to expression the core of Christianity, which is the paschal mystery."

19. See Zimmerman, *Liturgy as Living Faith*, 12–13, for a discussion of the levels of meaning of *zkr* in Deuteronomy and the significance of *zkr*, which leads to action.

actors or observers, beyond the doing of the dramatization itself. In the case of liturgical enactment, however, the consequence of ontological remembrance is existential action where being and doing interpenetrate. Every liturgical enactment enables us to see ourselves more clearly as Body of Christ (being) and graces us to choose more fully how we will act in the world as that Body (doing).

Liturgy is the ritual enactment and reaffirmation of Christian identity as Body of Christ engaging in and being engaged by the paschal mystery. The essential core of Christian liturgy, its ontological referent, and its structural underpinning is the paschal mystery. This understanding is the primary liturgical recovery of Vatican II and is the deepest meaning of *Sacrosanctum Concilium's* liturgical mandate concerning full, conscious, and active participation of all the faithful in the liturgy. Because of and through liturgy we can encounter the paschal mystery as our own and can appropriate its challenges into our daily living. As "summit toward which the activity of the Church is directed" and "fountain from which all her power flows,"[20] liturgy both grounds our identity as Body of Christ, and leads us toward the eschatological fulfillment of that identity.[21]

Concept of Time

Paul Ricoeur's investigations into time and narrativity help us understand how both liturgy and Christian living enact in the present the historically past Christ event.[22] Ricoeur builds his speculations about time on the reflections of Augustine found in the *Confessions*.[23] For Augustine the past that is no longer and the future that has not yet come to be are nonexistent; only the present is. All three temporalities nonetheless do exist in the soul as memory (past), attention (present), and expectation (future). Thus, for Augustine, time in all its modes exists as a threefold present: the "present of things past, the present of things present, and a present of things future."[24]

Augustine uses the recitation of a psalm to exemplify his point:

20. *SC*, no. 10.

21. Thus, Pius XII could rightly say in *Mediator Dei* (*Acta Apostolicae Sedis* 39:14 [1947]): no. 29, that the most pressing duty of Christians is to live the liturgical life.

22. See Zimmerman, "Paschal Mystery—Whose Mystery?"

23. Augustine, *Confessions* XI, 14:17–28:37; trans. taken from *Nicene and Post-Nicene Fathers*, vol. 1, ed. Philip Schaff (Grand Rapids, MI: Eerdmans, 1974 rpt.).

24. Augustine, *Confessions* XI, 20:26.

I am about to repeat a psalm that I know. Before I begin, my attention is extended to the whole; but when I have begun, as much of it as becomes past by my saying it is extended in my memory; and the life of this action of mine is divided between my memory, on account of what I have repeated, and my expectation, on account of what I am about to repeat; yet my consideration is present with me, through which that which was future may be carried over so that it may become past. Which the more it is done and repeated, by so much (expectation being shortened) the memory is enlarged, until the whole expectation be exhausted, when that whole action being ended shall have passed into memory. And what takes place in the entire psalm, takes place also in each individual part of it, and in each individual syllable: this holds in the longer action, of which that psalm is perchance a portion; the same holds in the whole life of man [sic], of which all the actions of man are parts; the same holds in the whole age of the sons of men, of which all the lives of men are parts.[25]

At the beginning of the recitation, all the psalm is in the future; as he prays, some of the psalm remains in the future while some passes over into the past. Yet because of memory and expectation, all the psalm continually exists in the present. Augustine shows us that time is not measured by external motion (as, for example, the movement of the sun through the day), but by the inward and fixed element of the mind. The crucial verb, then, is not "'to pass' (*transire*) but 'to remain' (*manet*)."[26] Augustine moves time beyond chronology by opening up a deeper temporality. Ricoeur develops Augustine's thinking by applying his dialectical approach: the three modalities of time—memory (past), attention (present), and expectation (future)—stand in dialectic tension with one another. Time is an action by which the mind actively creates the presence of the past, the present, and the future.

This analysis throws new light on our understanding of liturgical time and participation in the paschal mystery. The Christ event stands both in the past historically and in the future in terms of the Second Coming. We live in the present between the past and the future modes of this event. Liturgical time is the dialectic of our present with the past and the future of the mystery of Christ. Liturgical time, then, is participatory action. What mediates the past and the future of the

25. Augustine, *Confessions* XI, 28:38.
26. Ricoeur, *Time and Narrative*, vol. 1, trans. Kathleen McLaughlin, and David Pellauer (Chicago and London: The University of Chicago Press, 1984) 18; quoted in Zimmerman, "Paschal Mystery—Whose Mystery?" 307.

12

Christ event is an integrating present that is the *action* of the baptized community engaging in the dialectic of Christian memory, attention, and expectation.[27] As an action in the present, liturgy unfolds in chronological time, but as an act of *anamnesis* liturgy opens up the deeper dynamic of time as our actualization in the present of the past and future dimensions of our identity and mission.

A Hermeneutics of Liturgical Enactment

The word "hermeneutic" comes from the god Hermes whose task was to carry messages from the other gods to human beings. In communicating these messages Hermes was swift and direct, but he could also be a thief, a trickster, and a bargainer. Negotiating with him, then, required the art of interpretation, that is, that art of perceiving the message, understanding its meaning, and making sense of its application to one's life.

We use Paul Ricoeur's textual hermeneutics here to elucidate how it is that liturgy enacts Christian identity and mission. Applying his method to the specific text which is liturgy ("text" here meaning not just what is written, such as, for example, the Sacramentary, but the whole rite as it is actually celebrated) enables us to understand how liturgy enacts past originary Christian events in present and future modes.

To begin, it is important to note that for Ricoeur "text" is broader than what is written and includes any enduring sign of human existence, such as works of art, music and dance, ritual and liturgy. All texts—rites, monuments, archives, artifacts, etc.—are documents of human existence and all participate in a dialectic of past, present, and future (that is, of the originary event that gave rise to the text, of the present context of the text user, and of the possibilities for actualization of new self-understanding opened up by the text). It is also important to note that "understanding" is not so much an intellectual activity having to do with ideas and concepts as it is an ontological activity having to do with self-understanding and self-actualization. Understanding is not a process of the mind alone; it is even more a process of the heart and the will.[28] Hermeneutics deals not only with how we interpret a "text" but also with how that "text" interprets us

27. Zimmerman, "Paschal Mystery—Whose Mystery?" 310–12.
28. Zimmerman, *Liturgy as Living Faith*, n. 3, 149.

by challenging our self-understanding and our way of living in the world.

Ricoeur's hermeneutic method encompasses three interpretative moments (participation, distanciation, appropriation) that establish a dynamic relationship between us and the text, leading to deeper understanding of the text. The three interpretative moments do not unfold chronologically, but are present as ongoing dialectics that act upon one another in such a way as to move us deeper into the meaning of the text (and therefore into self-understanding and self-actualization).

Participation. Participation is a moment of "pre-understanding" originating from our immersion in being as mediated through a particular tradition.[29] Such pre-understanding derives from two perspectives, that of belonging and that of communication. Belonging is our preconscious sense that our very being belongs to being and to Being; we apprehend that we belong to the whole of what is. Through communication we experience this belonging as intersubjective and intratemporal. Belonging is apprehended through the cultural monuments—texts, rites, documents, archives, etc.—that comprise tradition. Tradition implies a certain connectedness with others and with history that is also a connectedness to ourselves. All interpretation takes place within a tradition that both enables communication of the originary events giving rise to the tradition and grounds our identity. This tradition establishes the parameters out of which our initial interpretation of a text is made; we construct meaning out of "guesses" among the possible meanings that the tradition suggests.

In terms of liturgy, we who live within the Christian tradition share through baptism an identity that immerses us in the paschal mystery and unites us ontologically with Christ and with one another as Body of Christ. Our interpretation of the text of Christian existence is shaped, then, by our self-understanding as Body of Christ. The originary event for the Christian tradition—the paschal mystery—is encapsulated in the present through liturgical enactment. From our participation in the accumulated meaning of liturgy throughout tradition and from our participation in Christian living, we bring pre-

29. For Ricoeur, lived experience is itself a "pre-comprehension of what is to be articulated" (S. Skousgaard, *Language and the Existence of Freedom: A Study in Paul Ricoeur's Philosophy of Will* [Washington, D.C.: University Press of America, 1979], 78), quoted in Zimmerman, *Liturgy as Language of Faith*, 88.

understanding to the liturgical celebration, implicitly grasping the reference to originary Christian events expressed in sacramental form.

Distanciation. While participation in a tradition grants us certain parameters for authentic interpretation, it is only the first moment of interpretation. Ricoeur's second methodic moment is distanciation. Standing in dialectic opposition to participation, distanciation is an *analytic* moment allowing us to step aside from the moment of belonging to reflect on its meaning and to uncover new possibilities for living that it offers. While participation is largely unconscious, distanciation is conscious, deliberate, interpretive activity. Without the deliberative, analytic activity of distanciation, the new possibilities for existence opened up by the text remain buried in the comfort zone of our already existing interpretations.

Distanciation is an interpretive moment directed toward the internal structure[30] of a text in itself (for example, a musical composition, a painting, a liturgical document, a given celebration of liturgy). And because every text is an objectification of the relation of belonging, its interpretation is immensely fruitful for our continued living of the tradition that produced the text. Disclosure of its depth structure, then, is fundamentally an analysis of human existence, for it arises from existence (participation) and moves toward renewed existence (appropriation), the third methodic moment.

In terms of liturgy, distanciation is the activity of interpretation directed toward disclosure of liturgy's deep structure. Liturgy is a concrete text that objectifies the originary event of the paschal mystery and our fundamental identity as Body of Christ. Authentic liturgical interpretation, then, yields greater understanding both of the paschal mystery and of Christian identity. One moment of this hermeneutic activity is scholarly study, but another moment is what we enter each time we engage in liturgical celebration. By entering into the objectification of the Christ event, which is liturgy, we open up new possibilities for appropriating it: we discover ourselves, both as we are and as we can become.

---

30. For Ricoeur structure means more than simply observable data (which belong to a "surface" structure). Zimmerman states, "'Structure' is a depth dynamic that makes something what it is. The closer we come to grasping a text's deep structure, the closer we come to entering the human existence documented by the text" (*Liturgy as Living Faith*, n. 6, 149).

Appropriation. Distanciation is dialectically related to participation in Christian existence because it opens up new possibilities for Christian living. The third interpretive moment, appropriation, stands in dialectic position on the other side of distanciation (and in turn becomes a new moment of participation). In the moment of appropriation, we choose among the many possibilities for living that distanciation opens up in order to make the meaning of the text our own. Distanciation allows us to encounter other possibilities opened up by the text and to choose new possibilities for our present situation. This very choosing is the moment of appropriation; our encounter with the text culminates in self-interpretation: we understand ourselves better, or differently, or perhaps even for the first time.[31]

Appropriation signifies a change in us which ultimately brings about a change in the world. Appropriation is the subjective counterpart to distanciation; it is not, however, response to the author but to the text, that is, to the world of possibilities that the text opens up. Moreover, appropriation gives precedence to the world projected by the text over any projection by us as reader onto the text. Appropriation requires a relinquishment of ego; it is defined by a loss of our old self in order to find and actualize a new self.

Liturgically, appropriation is our choosing new ways of living out the paschal mystery in our daily Christian living. Interpreting the originary event, which liturgical celebration makes present in objectified form, we see afresh our identity and mission as Body of Christ. What we interpret and reappropriate is Christian self-understanding; what we choose is a new way of being Christian. This new way of being which grace continually creates is *ourselves as Body of Christ*, and every moment of appropriation becomes a new moment of participation. The pathway to new appropriation of self is always relinquishment of old self-understandings. For grace to work we must consciously choose to let go of self. We must die in order to rise.

Application to liturgy. Ricoeur's textual hermeneutics offer us a way to understand how liturgy enacts in the present and for the future the originary paschal mystery event. Liturgy is a text of Christian ex-

---

31. Zimmerman, *Liturgy as Living Faith*, 43: "The ultimate goal of interpretation is a new self who lives a new human existence with new situations and new possibilities. The interpretive process proceeds from a participation in human existence (objectified as a "text") to a distanciation from existence in order to recognize new possibilities for appropriation."

istence arising from the originary paschal mystery event. Because of our participation in Christian existence, we pre-understand both the text and its originary event (participation). The celebration of liturgy allows us to encounter the meaning of this originary event in terms of its possibilities for our present situation (distanciation). The ritual encounter with the paschal mystery generates new levels of self-understanding and self-actualization of Christian identity and mission (appropriation). Between the past of the originary event and lived tradition and the future of new ways of configuring that tradition stands the present of liturgical enactment, itself generated by the past and in turn generative of the future.

Specifically, liturgy (our ritual enactment of the paschal mystery) and Christian living (our lived enactment of that mystery) bear the same deep structure, that of the dialectic tension between soteriology and eschatology. As ritual enactment, liturgy provides the moment of distanciation in which the paschal mystery dialectic of soteriology and eschatology is made available for our interpretation. Our daily Christian living then becomes a new appropriation of that mystery as lived enactment. The two forms of enactment—liturgy and daily living—continually interact with one another to shape ever-deepening understanding of Christian identity as participation in the originary paschal mystery event.[32]

Liturgy and Christian living are the dialectic poles of an ongoing interpretative engagement in identity (Body of Christ) and meaningful action (paschal mystery), an engagement that constantly and progressively deepens our self-understanding and transforms our behavior. This means three things. First, it means that all Christian living is a reflection of a previous reading of liturgy. Second, it means that every celebration of liturgy re-figures the past as a fresh beginning. Third, it means that *"Christian living is the content of liturgy."*[33] Liturgy and

32. In light of Ricoeur's assertion that all texts are documents of human existence that carry the possibility of transforming present and future self-understanding, we could say that the yearly dramatization of Washington's crossing of the Delaware (see above) is in fact enactment. By its being a text encountered in a present situation, it carries new possibilities for self-understanding and self-actualization. However, we wish to reserve a cultic specificity to the term enactment. Enactment is cultic encounter with "texts" that are originary to a community's identity, paradigmatic for all time, and eschatological in import. Not every text can be enacted in this cultic sense (see above).

33. Zimmerman, *Liturgy as Living Faith*, xi (italics original).

Christian living bear the same ontological referent. Liturgy is not an activity isolated from the rest of life; rather, liturgy is life.

Analysis of the Eucharistic Rite[34]

Analyzing the surface structure of a liturgical rite provides a way to uncover the deep structure that underlies the rite. The term "deep structure" is drawn from the field of linguistic analysis and refers to the identity that makes a thing or text what it is. This identity is "not-at-hand," that is, it is not readily available to sense perception, but is disclosed through the surface structures, the "at-hand" phenomena that yield access to a thing's deep structure. Deep structure is abiding and defining; surface structures are the variable "at-hand" clues to this abiding "not-at-hand" identity.

The broad surface structure of the eucharistic rite is fourfold: introductory rites, Liturgy of the Word, Liturgy of the Eucharist, and concluding rite. The introductory rites bracket the demands of daily Christian living so that we may enter ritual activity. Through these introductory rites God calls us to ritual presence.

The Liturgy of the Word is the first major structural element of the rite. Its climax is the proclamation of the gospel. This is evidenced through ritual elements such as our posture of standing, our responses before and after the proclamation, and our singing of the gospel acclamation. What we acclaim in the gospel proclamation is the *"personal Presence* of the One being proclaimed."[35] The divine Presence who called us to presence in the introductory rites becomes a living, personal Presence showing us here and now what it means for us to be the Body of Christ. The proclamation of the gospel confronts us with the Ideal whom, as Body of Christ, we are called to become. The Liturgy of the Word, then, draws us into an intensified divine Presence and an intensified self-presence that is soteriological in function as the person of Christ present in the gospel calls us to new possibilities of being his Body in the world.

In the Liturgy of the Eucharist, the second major structural element of the rite, Ideal Presence becomes Real Presence. Through our recitation of the narrative of salvation (eucharistic prayer) and our procession to the messianic table, we recognize that we already are, truly and

34. I am indebted to Zimmerman here for this analysis that she details in ch. 7 of *Liturgy as Living Faith*.

35. Zimmerman, *Liturgy as Living Faith*, 106; italics original.

fully, the Body of Christ. The Liturgy of the Eucharist is an eschato-logical moment: it celebrates who we already are and invites us to rest in the joy of that becoming.

The very soteriological-eschatological dialectic that characterizes both the paschal mystery and its ritual enactment in liturgy is cap-tured, then, in the tension between the Liturgy of the Word and the Liturgy of the Eucharist, that is, in the tension between our confronta-tion with the Ideal we are called to become and God's fulfillment of that Ideal in the messianic banquet. Our pre-understanding is chal-lenged by our encounter in the gospel with the Ideal who is Christ, and we face the not-yetness of our human struggle to be the Body of Christ. The liturgy does not leave us there, however, but invites us forward into the originary story (the eucharistic prayer) and the reaffirmation that we already fully are the Body of Christ: it is ourselves we come to recognize in the breaking of the bread.[36] Thus the totality of the mystery—both the dying and the rising, both the not-yetness of our salvation and the already of our redemption—are fully present in the ritual enactment of who we are and who we are meant to be.

The concluding rite is a moment of recognition on our part that we have become "for others."[37] We are sent on our way with renewed self-understanding, ready to live in a way that makes a difference in the world. Together the introductory and concluding rites bracket the ritual moment, allowing us to set aside our participation in Christian living and enter ritual enactment of our identity, and sending us back into living with a new appropriation of what this identity means. What has been recovered is our self-understanding that the dialectic between soteriology and eschatology, between the "not yet" of our un-completed conformity to Christ and the "already" of our grace-given union with him that unfolds as the deep structure of the rite, is the text of our own Christian lives.

36. Thus Augustine could write: "If you are to understand what it means to be the Body of Christ, hear what Paul has to say: 'Now you are the body of Christ and individually members of it' (1 Cor 12:27). If you are the body of Christ and members of it, then it is that mystery which is placed on the Lord's table: you receive the mystery, which is to say the Body of Christ, your very self. You answer Amen to who you are and in the answer you embrace your-self. You hear Body of Christ and answer Amen. Be a member of Christ's body, that your Amen will be true" (Sermon 272 [Migne, PL, vol. 38] 1247; transla-tion by Zimmerman, *Liturgy as Living Faith*, 101).

37. Zimmerman, *Liturgy as Living Faith*, 109–10.

Analysis of the surface structure of the eucharistic rite reveals a deep structure that is the paschal mystery. The import of such disclosure is significant, for if the deep structure of liturgy is the paschal mystery, then the deep structure of liturgy is a dialectical unfolding of the tension between soteriology and eschatology. In other words, the dialectic that defines the paschal mystery also defines the ritual enactment of that mystery.

Dynamic of Presence. Analysis of the surface structure of the eucharistic rite further reveals that what draws the disparate elements of the rite into a single, unified, and complete action is an unfolding dynamic of presence, initiated by God and responded to by the assembly gathered for worship.[38] This dynamic begins with the Divine Presence calling us to cultic presence through the introductory rites. The very action of the introductory rites constitutes us as community by transforming our sense of "I" to a sense of "self-in-community."[39] Each of us brings to the gathering an individualized awareness of participation in Christian existence. The introductory rites transform these singularized self-understandings into communal self-understanding so that we recognize our identity as Body of Christ gathered to enact the paschal mystery. This transformation of self-awareness occurs at God's initiative. Cultic presence is presence to the God who calls and presence to one another as the community gathered by God into the one body of the church.

The Liturgy of the Word introduces a shift in the enactment as our focus moves from several persons (God, presider, assembly) to one (reader); our posture switches from standing to sitting and standing; our attention turns from presider's chair to ambo; and our activity changes from preparation to receptivity. The complex of actions as a whole reveals that the entire Liturgy of the Word centers on the word that is proclaimed, and particularly on the gospel. Every action of the Liturgy of the Word either leads up to or flows from the gospel understood as the proclamation of a living Person present in such a way that the word becomes relevant for this particular community in this particular time.

The Liturgy of the Word reveals Christ as the Ideal Presence whom we are in the process of becoming. The proclamation makes Christ present in such a way that he can be encountered by us here and now,

38. Zimmerman, *Liturgy as Language of Faith*, 180.
39. Ibid., 181.

and the very action of the Liturgy of the Word enables this encounter. Through our public assent, ritualized in posture and acclamation, we unite ourselves with the One being proclaimed. Christ is personally present in this proclamation, and so are we.

The Liturgy of the Eucharist introduces a further shift in the enactment as our focus turns from ambo to altar, and from Lectionary to bread and wine; our activity changes from receptivity back to preparation; and our engagement changes from active listening to active offering. Structurally, the eucharistic prayer is the central point around which the action is organized. The rites of preparing the gifts and of Communion frame this central section. Our actions of offering gifts and of eating and drinking the Body and Blood of Christ occur, then, in the context of the telling of the story of salvation. In this narration we encounter anew God's saving action in our favor. In the Communion rite we consume the Body and Blood of the one who brings salvation, and self-in-community is transformed into self-in-community-in-Christ: "Human presence and divine presence are commingled in . . . the fullness of Presence to presence."[40]

The concluding rite instigates a final shift in enactment to blessing and dismissal. The dismissal sends each member of the assembly forth to praise God by doing good works.[41] The dismissal calls us to affirm what we have just celebrated in the eucharistic action through a life that reflects its meaning. What we affirm at this point is not something taking place in the concluding rite itself, but the whole action that has preceded and will follow it. All the elements of the eucharistic rite are structured to lead to this final "Amen" on our part. To what are we saying "Amen"? Nothing less than our decision to appropriate possibilities for Christian living opened up by our having entered once again into God's Presence and been reminded that we are the Presence of Christ visible in the world today.

In the Liturgy of the Eucharist we celebrate our real Presence as Body of Christ. Through the blessing and dismissal of the concluding rite we are sent forth with new self-understanding to be this Presence for others. "Presence, then, is a key not only to understanding the deep dynamic of Eucharist but is also a key to how we live the Paschal Mystery in our daily lives."[42] The dynamic of action that the eucharistic

---

40. Ibid., 183.
41. *General Instruction of the Roman Missal 2002*, no. 90.
42. Zimmerman, *Liturgy as Living Faith*, 110.

liturgy unfolds is that of the interpenetration of divine and human presence as God makes Godself known and we take on that Godself in becoming Christ.

Liturgy is, then, a ritual in and through which human presence is given over to Divine Presence. The purpose of all liturgy is that we, the community of the baptized, transform our self-understanding and our mode of living. Ultimately, we come to see ourselves as God's Presence in the world, and choose to act accordingly. The deep structure of both liturgy and Christian living is the paschal mystery tension between soteriology and eschatology, between the not-yetness of human sin and weakness and the already of human gracefulness and glory. In both liturgy and life, what reveals the mystery and its power is the dynamic of personal presence, the ever-Presence of God and the becoming-ever-more-faithful presence of the Body of Christ.

Chapter 2

Our Experience of Sound, Music, and Song

All of us experience sound, music, and song as normal aspects of human living. We are surrounded by sounds in many forms, some pleasant and others strident, some attended to and others ignored, some generated by ourselves and others initiated by outside persons and sources. We use music as a means of entertainment, for purposes of relaxation, as part of our worship, and sometimes just as background for other more focused activities. We participate in song either directly or vicariously. We take all these phenomena for granted. In order to understand more fully the role music and song is meant to play in liturgical celebration, however, we need to take a deeper look at their nature, their meaning, and their impact on us. In the following pages we explore how sound reveals presence, binds interiorities, and manifests power; how music acts as a mode of revelation, participation, and relationship; and how sound, voice, and song reveal an interaction of force and resistance playing itself out within a changing center-periphery relationship between self and other.

DYNAMICS OF SOUND[1]

Sound Reveals Presence

All sound, even what can be classified as simply noise, registers itself in our consciousness as presence. Even when unseen or invisible or coming from a distance, we perceive this presence as very real and existential. The creek on the far side of the forest is present to us through its babbling. The two-year-old in the apartment next door becomes jarringly present in our living room when she shouts an

---

1. I am indebted for the insights here to Walter J. Ong, SJ, *The Presence of the Word: Some Prolegomena for Cultural and Religious History* (New Haven and London: Yale University Press, 1967); hereafter referred to as *Presence*; *Orality and Literacy: The Technologizing of the Word* (London: Methuen, 1982; rpt., London and New York: Routledge, 1988); hereafter referred to as *Orality*.

adamant "no!" Moreover, the presence sound conveys comes to us as a simultaneity. Visual space allows only one perspective at a time, and that head-on, but acoustic space diffuses itself around our bodies. We hear what is in front, what is behind, what is at either side, what is above, and what is below all at once. Sound envelops us in multi-dimensional presence.[2]

When the sound enveloping us is word, what we are encountering is the presence of person, and this is person as real, existential, here-and-now. Such presence is not accidental or arbitrary. Word is an actu-ality coming from a region to which no outsider has entry. When word is uttered, what sallies forth is a unique and hidden "I" that can come out of no other consciousness. To speak, then, is to choose to make oneself present and to hear is to admit the presence of this other into our own consciousness.

Sound Binds Interiorities

The sound a body projects is the consequence of interior properties and relationships. Sound reveals this hidden interiority. The appear-ance of a violin, for example, tells us nothing about its true value; only its sound can reveal the quality of the wood from which it is made and the condition and tension of its strings.

Sound reveals interiority in a way that our other senses cannot. Sight perceives only the light reflected from the surface of a thing. What sight perceives as depth is actually only a series of surfaces. When we notice, for example, that the rows of chairs in an auditorium seem to diminish in size the farther back we look into the room, it is not the "interiority" of the room we are seeing but the vanishing per-spective of objects in the room. Touch can perceive interiority but only if it invades or destroys a thing. To discern whether a box is empty, for example, we must tear it apart. Only sound can register the interior-ity of a thing without violating it; we simply rap on the box to discern

2. Ong, *Presence*, 129; also, 130: "Being in is what we experience in a world of sound." See also *Orality*, 72: "Vision comes to a human being from one direction at a time: to look at a room or a landscape, I must move my eyes around from one part to another. When I hear, however, I gather sound si-multaneously from every direction at once: I am at the center of my auditory world, which envelops me, establishing me at a kind of core of sensation and existence."

whether or not it is empty, or shake it to get some idea of what it contains.[3]

Sound not only reveals interiority, it binds interiorities together. Sound comes to us as a series of physical waves that set off reciprocating vibrations within the interior of every object they touch, stimulating a response, even when this is unwitting or across a great distance. To hear a sound, then, is to participate in the interiority of the source of that sound. This participation from the inside out, so to speak, dissipates our sense of separateness from the source of the sound. Sound binds together interiorities that would otherwise be unknown to, hidden from, and disconnected from one another.

When the sound operating in acoustic space is that of word, what becomes bound together are the conscious interiors—"the most interior of interiors"[4]—of human beings. Words both manifest disparate consciousnesses and bind these consciousnesses together. For this reason, word plays a privileged role in human interrelating; it is the sounding cement of community.

Sound Manifests Exercise of Power

Part of what we perceive in the actuality of sound is the use of power, and it is power being employed in the here-and-now. The babbling of the creek discloses the here-and-now force of water in motion. The "no!" of the toddler reveals the here-and-now exertion of this child's diaphragm and lungs. The presence sound reveals is not passive, then, but is always a presence exercising power.

When the sound we hear is word, the power exhibited goes far beyond the physical musculature involved in its production. Word reveals power in the act of determining both self and world. The "no!" of that toddler, for example, manifests the efforts of a fledgling self

3. Don Ihde, *Listening and Voice: A Phenomenology of Sound* (Athens: Ohio University Press, 1976), hereafter referred to as *Listening and Voice*, points to this as one of the everyday significations of sound we commonly employ to penetrate beneath the surface of a thing without breaking it open (*Listening and Voice*, 70). We thump on a melon, for example, to determine its ripeness. He further states: "[I]t is with the hearing of interiors that the possibilities of listening begin to open the way to those aspects which lie at the horizons of all visualist thinking, because with the hearing of interiors the auditory capacity of making present the *invisible* begins to stand out dramatically" (70); italics original.

4. Ong, *Presence*, 163. For Ong, persons are "pure interiors" (126).

to wield influence over her environment. This is why oral societies conceive of language as a mode of action. Words have power because sound by nature signals the use of power. Thus, the Hebrew notion of word (*dabar*) as event.[5] The divine word commanded, "Let it be!" and the world sprang into existence. Christ commanded, "Lazarus, come forth!" and one who was dead sprang back to life.

Word manifests power because it is event. When we give voice, then, we *become event*. We become presence bursting into the consciousness of the other as real, existential, powerful, and effective.

PURPOSE OF MUSIC[6]

Music Reveals the Nature of Reality

What gives tones their musical meaning is their dynamic quality. This dynamic quality is not a physical component that can be recorded in a laboratory (such as, for example, amplitude, pitch, or duration), but an intangible property that is nonetheless real and definitive: "[I]n the entire range of music no such thing as 'the tone E' or 'the tone A' occurs; what occurs is always and only the tone E *with a particular dynamic quality*, the tone a *with a different dynamic quality*. The dynamic quality, not the pitch, makes the tone a musical fact."[7] Furthermore, this dynamic is relational: a tone heard by itself has no dynamism, but a tone in a melody or as part of a diatonic scale is heard as a complex of relational pulls away from and toward other tones. This dynamism is nonmaterial, intangible, yet "alive," and it is this nonphysical dynamism that defines the essential meaning of a musical tone.

5. Ihde states: "The creative power of the Hebrew God is *word* which is spoken forth as power: *from word comes the world*. And although God may hide himself from the eye, he reveals himself in word which is also event in spite of the invisibility of his being" (*Listening and Voice*, 15; italics original). See also Edward Foley, *Foundations of Christian Music: The Music of Pre-Constantinian Christianity* (Collegeville, MN: Liturgical Press, 1996), who points out that for first-century Jews and early Christians hearing was believing; for them "[s]ound events were the prime mediator of presence and truth" (6).

6. For my insights here I am indebted to Victor Zuckerkandl, *Sound and Symbol: Music and the External World*, trans. Willard R. Trask (New York: Pantheon Books, 1956; Princeton: Princeton/Bollingen 1969; 1973); hereafter referred to as *External World*; *Man the Musician: Sound and Symbol*, vol. 2, trans. Norbert Guterman (Princeton University Press, 1973; Princeton/Bollingen, 1976); hereafter referred to as *Man the Musician*.

7. Zuckerkandl, *External World*, 91; italics original.

Musical hearing of this dynamic energy teaches us that the world is comprised of more than the tangible. The activity of our senses engages us with the materiality of the world. The data given by each of our senses is always palpably tied to the objective world: what is seen, for example, is not light or colors, but a mauve and golden sunset; what is tasted is not flavor, but the tartness of an apple. Musical hearing, however, is different, for tone is not the sensation of a physical thing. Language itself makes this distinction: "[W]e say, The leaf is green, the wall is smooth, the honey tastes sweet; but we do not say, The string is G, or the flute sounds D-ish."[8]

The dynamic events that are musical tones are conveyed through physical events—vibrations in the air, stimulation of our organs of hearing, responses of the nervous system—but they are not contained in these physical events. Moreover, the forces acting in music leave no trace in the physical events that convey them. What we learn from musical hearing, then, is that there is more to the world than what meets the eye.[9] Because hearing dynamic qualities in music is a direct perception of nonmaterial events through the medium of material events, musical hearing reveals that the two modes of existence—outer and inner, material and nonmaterial, tangible and intangible—are not closed off from one another but are the interpenetrating, double aspects of one, same world.[10] Musical hearing discloses this interrelationship because it simultaneously perceives, integrates, and recognizes as real a tone's outer acoustic properties and its inner dynamic energy. The differentiation between "inner" and "outer" is not abrogated, but their interrelatedness is clarified as the barrier between them is dissolved by the realization that this barrier is, in fact, nonexistent. What we perceive through musical hearing is the nature of the universe as

8. Ibid., 70–71.

9. This capacity of hearing to reveal the hidden dimension of reality is the motivation behind Ihde's development of an ontology of the auditory, which, like Zuckerkandl's work, is rooted in a phenomenology of auditory experience (*Listening and Voice*, 15); "*It is to the invisible that listening may attend*"(14; italics original); "[a]ny inquiry into the auditory is also an inquiry into the invisible. Listening makes the invisible *present* . . ." (51; italics original).

10. Zuckerkandl, *Man the Musician*, 158: "In music, the ear is not situated between two radically different worlds, separated by an unbridgeable gulf; rather, the events on this side of the sense organ (if one may put it this way) do not differ in kind from the events on the other side" (see also, *External World*, 366).

aggregate of the tangible and the intangible. Music that comes from the outer world reveals the inner world of reality, of things, of words, of identity, of time, motion, and space:

> [I]n music we *experience the world*. . . . Its unique significance for our thinking, for our understanding of the world, does not, then, lie in its leading to otherwise inaccessible insights. But what, elsewhere, can be made accessible only by laborious speculation, and then only uncertainly and insecurely—so that it always remains open to doubt, opposition, and rejection—music brings us patently. In music, what other phenomena conceal itself becomes phenomenon; in music, what is inmost to the world is turned outward.[11]

Music Catalyzes Participation

When human beings sing together in situations such as religious rites, social or political events, and practical work situations (for example, laborers at a common task), their singing breaks down the barriers that separate self from others, from things, and from actions.[12] In this musical crossing of barriers the self is not abandoned, however, but enlarged as focus on self as separate and individual is replaced by awareness of self as connected and communal.[13] The true purpose of musical tones is this exchange of separation for participation and the deepest purpose of song is the transformation of separation and opposition into partnership and collaboration.[14]

What is significant here is that the tones themselves are the medium that bring about this change. Tones and words are alike in that the "being in" of their meaning is nonmaterial. But the relationships between word and meaning and tone and meaning differ in that for the former the meaning (the thing signified) is independent of the word, whereas for the latter tone and meaning cannot be separated. Words indicate things beyond themselves, but what a word contains is only

---

11. Zuckerkandl, *External World*, 348; italics original. Also, 147: "We *see* the rind, or, under special conditions, *through* the rind, but [through music] we *hear* the core of this world;" italics original.

12. Zuckerkandl, *Man the Musician*, 23–25.

13. Ibid., 30: "The singer remains what he is, but his self is enlarged, his vital range is extended: being what he is he can now, without losing his identity, be with what he is not; and the other, being what it is, can, without losing its identity, be with him."

14. Zuckerkandl, *Man the Musician*, 30.

the indicating, not the thing indicated. Musical tones also point to something; their meaning, however, lies not in what they point to, but *"in the pointing itself."*[15] A tone is not separate from its meaning—in the very act of pointing the tone constitutes itself: being and reference are synonymous.[16]

Because with tones being and reference are synonymous, signifier and signified are one and subject and object can stand together. By contrast, words set up a separation between subject and object: what the word names becomes object, separate from the name. In like fashion, the namer becomes subject, separate from what has been named. Because tones, on the other hand, do not refer to anything outside themselves but contain within themselves the full and actual presence of their meaning, tones lead into themselves rather than away from themselves. In the self-possession and projection of their meaning, tones create a loop that pulls the singers and the things sung about into its centripetal arc.[17] Music abrogates the separations words create between signifier and signified, and between speaker and thing spoken about.

Music not only breaches the barrier between speaker and thing spoken about; it also overcomes the oppositional nature of interchange between speaker and hearer. Both song and speech employ words, but speaking sets up confrontational differences between the speaker and the one spoken to. The interlocutors face one another as distinct individuals, tossing words back and forth across the invisible net that delimits the nature of their discourse. In singing, however, individuals come together in a single identity, that of the group. Rather than facing off, they face the same direction.[18]

15. Zuckerkandl, *External World*, 68; italics original.

16. Ibid., 68: tones do more than signify meaning, they are the "complete, actual presence" of the meaning; "[t]ones . . . have completely absorbed their meaning into themselves and discharge it upon the hearer directly in their sound." Also, 371: "Certainly, the being of words could be characterized in the same way; but *we* have created words to the end of saying or signifying, *we* have given them their meanings; whereas, in tones, saying, meaning exists *by nature*"; italics original. See also *Man the Musician*, 117.

17. "By means of the tones, the speaker goes out to the things, brings the things from outside within himself [*sic*], so that they are no longer 'the other,' something alien that he is not, but the other and his own in one." Zuckerkandl, *Man the Musician*, 29.

18. "Whereas words turn people toward each other, as it were, make them look at each other, tones turn them all in the same direction: everyone follows

Music, then, reveals the fundamental togetherness in the being of things: subject and object stand together, self and other face the same direction. Tones reveal that under the differences that words identify exists a layer in which all things have a common rootedness, and from which they derive a common nourishment. All diversity arises from the same deep essence; all the layers, aspects, and differentiations of existence share a single birthing place and a common destiny. Beneath diversity exists a more fundamental unity, and it is this unity that is the very source of the being-ness of differentiation. Discovering and participating in the fundamental unity of all the differentiated elements of being is the primordial motivation for song:

> [P]eople sing in order to make sure, through direct experience, of their existence in a layer of reality different from the one in which they encounter each other and things as speakers, as facing one another and separate from one another—in order to be aware of their existence on a plane where distinction and separation of man and man [sic], man and thing, thing and thing give way to unity, to authentic togetherness.[19]

Experiencing self and others as co-participants in the fundamental unity of all being requires that we traverse the frontiers that seem to separate us. The essential nature of music is this very crossing. Through no other medium does this crossing occur with such immediacy and directness.

Music Clarifies the Nature of Time
To hear music is to think not only in time but with time; even more, it is to think time itself.[20] And what is this time which is thought? Two commonly accepted frameworks for defining time are, first, as the

----

the tones on their way out and on their way back. The moment tones resound, the situation where one party faces another is transmuted into a situation of togetherness, the many distinct individuals into the one group" (Zuckerkandl, *Man the Musician*, 28).

19. Zuckerkandl, *Man the Musician*, 42.

20. With music "one thinks not in time but with time; indeed, one thinks time itself in the form of tones, the only form in which time can be thought." Zuckerkandl, *Man the Musician*, 303; also, 347: "Tone is more than an audible event that occurs in time: it is audible time." Also, *External World*, 152: "[M]usic reveals existence as the flow of time. . . . Indeed, there is hardly a phenomenon that can tell us more about time and temporality than can music."

demarcation of past, present, and future and, second, as the counting of hours, minutes, and seconds. The first framework—time as demarcation of past, present, and future—raises more uncertainty than clarity about time, for its three divisions are in constant flux, the future continually becoming the present that is continually becoming the past. This approach leaves us in the precarious position of balancing ourselves on the hairline between two realms of nonbeing.

In musical hearing, however, we discover the simultaneity of the three modes of time through an immersion in the immediacy and fullness of the present. When we hear a melody, for example, we do not hear first one tone, then another, then another, and so on in isolated succession. Rather, with each tone we hear the totality of its relationships with the other tones, both those sounding before and those coming after. What is significant, however, is that musical hearing does not recognize the present tone's dynamic quality because the ear recalls past tones and anticipates future ones. We do not hear melody in fragmented pieces, but holistically. We hear what is, what has been, and what will be as a simultaneity.

The key is in grasping the *now* of music. Musical meter, for example, is "a present in which 'now,' 'not yet,' and 'no more' are given together, in the most intimate interpenetration and with equal immediacy."[21] In musical meter the past requires no remembering and future no foreseeing because both are already, immediately, and fully present within each now moment of the meter. Moreover, the presence of past and future within the now of meter's flow does not depend upon human psychological powers of remembering and foreseeing: it is not memory that stores the past, but *time itself*, not foreknowledge that anticipates the future, but *time itself.*[22]

This same interpenetration of past, present, and future exists in the hearing of tone. Every tone sounds not only itself but also its relationship with what has been sounded and with what is yet to be sounded. Because every tone contains within itself all its dynamic meaning, all its movement away from and toward, it holds and dispels upon our ear in the immediacy of its present sounding all its past and all its

21. Zuckerkandl, *External World*, 227–28.

22. Ibid., 228; italics original. For an expansion of Zuckerkandl's analysis of meter and time, see Jeremy S. Begbie, *Theology, Music and Time* (Cambridge: Cambridge University Press, 2000), 37–44.

future. To hear music, then, is to discover the essence of time: that it is a storing of itself.[23]

We have already pointed out that melody is a temporal *Gestalt*, all its parts given in one immediate experience. As with meter and tone, this presence of the past and the future in the now is not a function of human remembering or foreseeing. In fact, when we dwell on past tones or imagine future ones we lose engagement with the melody; we cease to hear it. Our experience of hearing melody reiterates the revelation that time stores itself, and that we need only enter the flow of music to experience and understand the essence of time.

The second common framework for defining time—as the counting of hours, minutes, and seconds—is an artificially established construct that measures not time but movement, that is, the amount of motion one body makes in relation to another as, for example, that the earth turns itself once in relation to the sun every twenty-four hours. The construct deals not with time, then, but with space.[24] Within this framework change creates time, that is, the turning of the earth on its axis produces the hours by which we calculate it. Examination of the time components of music (meter and rhythm), however, leads us to the opposite conclusion: time creates change.[25] The temporal succession through which tones unfold in music is not simply flux, but a combination of flux and cycle, which is wave. The active forces in this wave produce meter and rhythm, and what beats as this wave is time: "The forces of the wave are forces of time—or better, are time as force."[26] What we experience in the rhythm of music and recognize as such is not some measurement of time, nor some analogue of time, but *time itself*.

Thus music discloses that time is not a philosophical construct, an idea for measuring or explaining change and motion, but is, in itself, an active force of existence. Rather than measuring events, *time produces events*.[27] Within the intellectual concept of time, forces of things *in* time (we often refer to these as "effects *of* time") are at work; for example, we note that over time heat melts snow. Time itself is thought to be inactive, even nonexistent, merely a way of measuring other forces.

23. Zuckerkandl, *External World*, 228.

24. Zuckerkandl, *Man the Musician*, 208–9.

25. See Zuckerkandl, *Man the Musician*, 184–85. See 157–200 for his complete, lengthy argumentation of this point.

26. Zuckerkandl, *Man the Musician*, 200.

27. Zuckerkandl, *External World*, 203–8; italics added.

Music, however, reveals that time itself is an active force that produces effects; meter and rhythm in music are not units of measurement, but products of and evidence of the forces of time acting in a dynamic field. The musician who sensitively phrases a performance of music understands this; so does the listener for whom such a performance "comes alive."

In the hearing of music, then, we discover that the present is not a line dividing past from future. Musical hearing is neither remembrance of the past nor foreknowledge of the future, but presence to and participation in the completeness of time in every present moment.[28] Musical hearing further reveals that time is not just an intellectual idea, nonexistent outside of philosophical thought. Rather, time is the active force of existence that creates change.

POWER OF SONG[29]

Three Fields of Human Action

Human beings operate within three basic fields of action, each bearing a unique configuration and standing in relation to the others in an order of increasing fluidity and decreasing rigidity in terms of boundaries between the self as center and all else as periphery.[30] Field 1 is the arena of physical space, where the physical body stands as the center and sight holds primacy in sense-initiated surveying of the periphery. The solidity of external objects is a determining factor in the mobility of the body, for it must push off from what is solid but cannot pass through it. Categories within the topology of Field 1 include inside-outside, withinness-withoutness, and separation-connection. These categories stand in oppositional rather than dialectical relationship; that is, a given external object, even along a changing continuum

28. Ann Landers reported this relevant anecdote about Arturo Toscanini: On the day Toscanini turned eighty, someone asked his son Walter what his father would consider his greatest achievement. The son answered that for his father there was no such thing. "Whatever he happens to be doing at the moment is the biggest thing in his life—whether it's conducting a symphony, or peeling an orange" (*Dayton Daily News* [March 4, 2000], 8C).

29. For material in this section I am indebted to David Burrows, *Sound, Speech and Music* (Amherst: University of Massachusetts Press, 1990).

30. We do not move through these Fields in sequence; rather, we move in and out of each somewhat randomly, and often operate within more than one, even all three, simultaneously.

of contiguity, is either one or the other (for example, inside or outside, separate or connected, left or right) in relation to the body, never both. Field 1 is sense limited, time and space specific, and bounded by the here and now. Moreover, it is limited to individuated awareness: what one person perceives from her or his angle is never the same as what another person perceives from a different angle.

Field 2 is the world of the mind (the realm of thought) where time and space are unspecific, where what is not here and now can be "seen," where the frame of reference is unlimited because the periphery is made up of the intangible psychical edges of ideas, dreams, memories, and inventions. Field 2 opens up reality beyond the borders of physical appearances. Although activity within this field takes place within the self and in the now, it is limited to neither, because in Field 2 the individual can go backward and forward in time and can pass, through discourse, into the conscious mental world of others. Shared awareness is possible. What does pose limits upon Field 2 activity, however, is the consensus of the community, that is, the rules of discourse, the syntax of language, and the social expectations of logical correspondence between what is thought and what is expressed.

Field 3 is the realm of the spirit[31] where the sense of self becomes contiguous with all reality, where peripheries no longer exist because everything becomes center. In Field 2, limits of the world of here and now are stretched to the edges of the capacity to think, to remember, to dream, and to imagine. In Field 3 all limits disappear as barriers between the center (self) and the periphery (other, world, cosmos) dissipate in an awareness of the oneness of self with the whole of things. This is the field natural to neonates and to mystics, but accessible to all persons through meditation, through ritual, and through participation in music and the arts. It is through the faculties of thought and speech that we enter Field 2 and come into contact with realities far beyond the remotest capabilities of our physical reach in Field 1. But it is through the avenues of ritual and art that we enter Field 3 and discover that even the most distant reality is very close to home, for here we encounter our oneness with all that is. Significant for our study here is that the most direct route into Field 3 is found through music.[32]

31. "Spirit" is used here by Burrows not as a theological term, but as "the sense of self as diffused through the full range of awareness" (*Sound*, 8).

32. Burrows never demonstrates the reality of Field 3; he simply asserts its existence through phenomenological description. Zuckerkandl's work gives

Differential Roles of Sound, Voice, and Song

Within each of the three fields of human action, sound bears increasing relevance. In Field 1, sight and vision are the primary modes through which we deal with what is other than self, but in Field 2 speech and hearing are the crucial functions that orient us in relation to what is other. Sight predominates in Field 1 because it provides us with a certitude about the position and direction of things that sound cannot give. This surety about the physical parameters of what is seen is the result of the straightforwardness of the light waves that bring the information to us. But herein also lies the limitation of sight, for it cannot perceive light waves blocked by an intervening object, such as a pillar or a wall. By contrast, sound waves billow around barriers and pass through walls, overlapping and interpenetrating one another along the way. Furthermore, sight arranges objects in a discrete order separated by their precise geographies: near-far, high-low, left-right. Sound, however, causes the topology of Field 1 to lose its discrete definitions because it enables objects and activities to interpenetrate.[33]

While both sight and sound are the major avenues through which we become aware of what is distant from the self, the two phenomena set up very different relationships with what is distant.[34] Sight draws us beyond ourselves to the object seen. Sound, on the other hand, moves toward us, entering our personal space with an intimacy that generates a sense of identity with the source of the sound. Sound engages involvement.[35] Moreover, this involvement cannot be dismissed;

---

support both to the notion of Field 3 and to music as doorway into that field and does so by assuming a metaphysical stance.

33. Ong discusses this phenomenon in terms of the multidimensionality of sound. Despite the fact that sound waves dissipate as instantly as they are generated, the world of sound has a depth and a plenitude that is absent from the plane of sight (*Presence*, 130).

34. See Ihde, *Listening and Voice*, 49–71, for a discussion of phenomenal overlap between the realms of sound and sight. Although markedly different in their modes of operation, sound and sight also share a similarity of style. While it is true that the sensory information given by sound is generally simultaneous, and that given by sight is sequential, sound is also sequential—the progression of a melody, for example, unfolds only sequentially—and sight is simultaneous—the meaning of a painting is immediately available to the eye in its totality.

35. Burrows, *Sound*, 16: "Sight draws me out, sound finds me here. . . . The bell is off over there; the ringing is here, and there, and all around,

we cannot ignore sound the way we can block vision (we can wink an eye but not an ear). This involvement with what is other can generate a sense of comfortable identification with the source of the sound or it can stimulate a feeling of alarm if the source is distant, hidden, or unrelated in size and shape to the impact the sound is making on us. Unlike sight, when sound enters our perception it is not appearance but something underneath and beyond appearance that impinges upon us.

Sight places us in a specific location and assures us of our grounding. Sound is likewise grounded because it issues from an embodied source. But sound always leaves this source behind.[36] When we are the source of the sound the result is a feeling of being both at place in our bodies and beyond our bodies. We become aware of being here and now while at the same time being over there and beyond. It is particularly when we are singing that we experience ourselves expanding into and filling whatever space is surrounding us.

The most intimate and powerful way we exploit the potential in sound is through voice.[37] Burrows offers a model for explaining the many uses of voice based on the interaction of force with resistance. All sound begins with a clash between a force and a resistance:

> [Sound] is a consequence of the activity of things and not of all their activity at that: only of activity that is resisted in certain ways. Only when things bump into other things or rub against them do we hear sounds; or it may be that what we hear is the air pushing itself past a resistance, as when it whistles past a cornice or the mouthpiece of a flute. Thudding and smashing result from the uncompromising impact of mass on mass. . . . When two masses grudgingly negotiate a way past each other we may hear rasping, creaking, and squealing. Things are not always coming up against each other in these ways. We can see them whether they move or not, but we can hear them only when they move . . .[38]

----

within me and without. While I listen the whole notion of separateness and distance fades as a perceptual issue." Sound is a "vibrant connective tissue" that involves us, consciously or not, in "what the source of the sound is going through" (24).

36. Burrows, *Sound*, 20. Localized at its inception in the body, sound becomes nonlocalized when it leaves the body, and continues to expand in the nonlocalized manner of sound waves.

37. Burrows, *Sound*, 12.

38. Ibid., 23.

Sound as voice is a paradigm of the interaction between the force of the self and the resistance of the world.[39] On the physical level, vocalization results from the resistance of the larynx to pressure exerted by breath being pushed out of the lungs by the diaphragm. On the level of social interaction, vocalization represents the ongoing struggle of the self to establish control over what is outside the self. In vocalization both the force and the resistance are internal to the body, as is the threshold of their confrontation, and this vocalization that begins as control over the larynx comes symbolically to represent control over the threshold between self and other. We use voice to stake out territorial claim over our environment and over the others who people it.[40]

Speech not only stretches the territory brought under the speaker's control, it also moves both speaker and hearer(s) into a new realm of coexistence, the realm of Field 2 where sound as word projects the interlocutors into the world of thought.[41] The result is a shared shift in orientation to what is not immediately here and now, with the potential to interpenetrate one another's imaginings, mental projections, dreams, and desires. Sound as speech enables us to hear one another think. Thus the same facility for language and speech through which we can assert claims to territoriality can also bond us with others in a sharing of territoriality. A new realm not only of thought but of communal living opens up. Moreover, because speech and conversation rove as randomly as the sound that produces them, unshackled by physical solidities, the communal realm they open up for us has a limitless horizon.[42]

39. Ibid., 30–31. There is a "parallel between the confrontation of breath with larynx that results in the sound of the voice, and that of the self with its world . . . the force with which air is exhaled from the lungs and the resistance it meets from the vocal folds mime the resistance offered by the world to the centrifugal energies of the self . . ." (12).

40. "[Because] the relationship between force and resistance at the sounding larynx mimes the corresponding relationship between self and other . . . vocalizing thus enacts a taking charge by proxy on the part of the self of its situation, and . . . addressing the resulting sound to listeners is a bid to resonate them with a token for that situation and so a bid for a measure of control over them" (Burrows, *Sound*, 41). See also 37.

41. Burrows, *Sound*, 41–49 and passim.

42. Ibid., 48. Burrows further suggests that the nature of sound determined the manner in which human speech evolved. It was sound's capability to detach itself from what was seen that led to language's ability to represent what

But speech is only one of two ways we produce vocal sounds with conscious intent to influence others. The other way is song, and this mode is the more captivating because it originates at a physiologically deeper place within the body—at the larynx as opposed to the tongue, teeth, and lips, where the phonemes of speech are produced.[43] This is so because vowels, which carry intonation, resonate farther back in the vocal track than consonants, which articulate the phonemes of speech. Where speech uses consonants to articulate phonemes and, therefore, verbal meaning, song uses vowels to articulate pitch, timbre, and resonance that are in themselves nonsemantic.[44]

Speaking articulates phonemes at the threshold of the mouth, but singing is a "musical articulation" of pitch and timbre generated at the larynx. Singing is a form of vocalization projected from deeper within the body. Because it originates at a deeper physical point in our vocalization mechanism, and because it uses the more fluid and flexible vowels, singing is naturally more resonant than speech. Singing fills us with a greater sense of self. In terms of the meeting between self and the world that vocalization mediates, singing has a deeper foothold on the side of self.

Singing, then, expresses an inherent solipsism. Paradoxically, it is this very self-awareness that enables singing done in concert to bind separate selves into a single identity. Babies "sing" before they speak. Their singing is characterized by a sense of being in union with all that exists—not, however, because they are aware of their individuation and choose to dialogue across the barriers between self and others. Speaking is the primary vehicle for such dialogue, but the newborn has not yet learned either how to use this tool or its necessity for survival. The baby is simply unaware of its difference and separation from the rest of the world. Ensemble singing returns us to this neonate

---

was unseen (49–52). Sound formed into speech became the avenue whereby the human community could seek out and represent unseen significances, for "the existence of symbols emancipated from appearance is an invitation to create further symbols for what could never have any appearance at all" (52).

43. Burrows, *Sound*, 60: "The claims on attention of phonemes formed at the upper end of the tubular cavity from which speech issues, and along with them the claims of referential meaning, fade in relation to those of the physically more deeply centered resonances of the larynx . . ." Burrows speaks here of speech and song as they are commonly understood in Western music and languages.

44. Burrows, *Sound*, 62–65.

worldview in which the self is contiguous with all that exists. Communal singing transforms individualism into the collectivity of a shared orientation and identity.[45]

A further reason why song transforms the center-periphery ratio of human awareness and action is the centripetal pull of music. Music, by virtue of its use of recurring rhythms and motifs, by virtue of its origins within the interiorities of persons and instruments, and by virtue of its nonsemantic reference,[46] is naturally centripetal, folding back upon itself and enfolding awareness around a single center. Its effect is the opposite of speech, which is naturally centrifugal, moving speaker and hearer away from the here and now to unseen worlds and from individualized perceptions to shared ideations. Speech expands awareness; music focuses it. Speech expands the awareness of possibilities ranging over past, present, and future; music focuses the awareness of presence in the present. In so doing, the horizon of those engaged in the music (either as performers or as listeners) is paradoxically expanded, for the communal focusing of awareness on a single center dissolves the experience of differences and separation among the participants. The sense of other as oppositional dissipates as we enter together into a shared new world. This centering capacity of music is the primary purpose of its invention and use: it stands as counterbalance to the centrifugal impulses of speech.

Both words and music generate a sense of presence and togetherness. Both share their progenitor's (sound) characteristic of obliterating the differentiations between inside and outside, between here and there, but music reaches the objective of instilling a quality of presence more quickly and more fully than does speech. Song centers presence and awareness more quickly than speech because song fuses the

45. Ibid., 68.

46. In the perennial debate about whether the locus of musical meaning lies within the music itself or outside it in some semantic reference, Burrows stands on the nonsemantic side of the issue: "[M]usic is not essentially in the business of representing things beyond itself" (*Sound*, 71); "music largely dispenses with the semantic component that is speech's reason for being" (89). For Burrows, "living the sound itself, in all its sectors and over all its time spans, is the root of its musical meaning" (89). Burrows calls this musical level of meaning "protosemiosis." See above for Zuckerkandl's stance, which is in agreement with Burrows. See also Begbie's lengthy discussion of this issue in *Theology, Music, and Time*, 11–28.

semantic use of sound (language) with its nonsemantic use (music).[47]
The analytic processes that the semantic nature of language discourse
set in motion and that necessarily include an element of defensiveness
in their investigation are subsumed into the nondefensive posture
of music-making. Singing opens up a resonant presence that allows
words to penetrate our being at a deeper level. This experience is particularly evident, for example, in plainsong chanting where speech
is so regulated and stylized that we enter an almost dissociated state
of awareness into which the words drop and diffuse themselves. All
genres of sung text, even those with highly varying rhythmic and
melodic components, have this capacity.

Center-Periphery Schema

As we move from one field of human action to another, the boundaries of the center-periphery relationship between self and nonself
shift. In Field 1 both center and periphery are fixed by the physical
dimensions of the self and its surrounding objects. The periphery
that self surveys is limited to what here-and-now reality can be perceived by the senses. Self (as body) stands in the center. Territoriality
is sharply defined and defended by the center (even when that "defense" is no more than turning one's body a step to the right in order
to avoid collision with a piece of furniture). Vision dominates because
of its capacity to clearly demarcate the distances and differences of
peripheral objects from the center.

In Field 2 the periphery to which the self relates expands via the
medium of thought. Past and future become available, as well as
nonsensible possibilities. Although the self still stands as center, this
self (as mind) can be carried elsewhere to the unlimited margins of
imagination. Moreover, through the use of sound as speech the self
can enter other personal centers of thought and imagination. The periphery expands. In Field 2 sound as voice spins attention away from
the center as speech articulates notions about what is not present, not
visible, even nonexistent. Thus the self tangles with ambiguities and

47. Music facilitates our ability to enter into its realm because its nonsemantic nature "involves one cognitive operation less than does understanding
speech" (Burrows, *Sound*, 88). Music does not demand the denotative and con-
notative translation that speech does. We simply take in the sound as sound.
"The text is there, as T. S. Eliot once said of the words of a poem, partly to
keep those parts of the mind and body responsible for words engaged while
the song goes about its deeper work" (73).

40

contingencies at the periphery and suffers a consequent uncertainty about identity and place within the scheme of things. Two dynamics occur, one being the dissipating of the center-periphery boundaries through the sharing of psychic territories as thought and discourse move the self out of the singularity of one mental landscape, the other being the reinforcement of energies toward the establishment of clearly delimited and defended boundaries. The sharing of territoriality that thought and voice enable is limited by the ways language is used to define and differentiate, demarcate and separate. Thus, there is a tension in Field 2 between the expansionist effects of thought and discourse and the urgent need to claim and defend private territory. Sound as speech is used on both sides of this tension.

In Field 3 (the world of music and of ritual), both the boundaries between center and periphery and the edges of the periphery itself dissipate because the self enters a realm of action where separation from nonself is replaced by an awareness of mystical, cosmic union with all that is. There are no borders; rather, there is only center and it is all in all. Territoriality becomes a nonissue; rather, the self (soul) experiences its place in the interrelatedness of all being.[48] In Field 3 voice becomes song, and the centripetal energies of music overcome the centrifugal tendencies of language. In Field 2 speech spins attention out away from the center because the thoughts it conveys are frequently not tied to here-and-now, sense-verifiable data. Speech is also used as a tool to extend and defend personal territory. In Field 3, however, speech as song shares in the "homecoming" tendency of music to pull all things toward the center. In both Fields it is sound's ability to unite and connect disparate bodies that is at play, but in the case of Field 2, sound as speech as frequently acts against connecting as in favor. In Field 3, however, the energy of sound as music moves in only one direction and that is homeward toward unity.

Interaction of Force and Resistance

In each field of human action the force-meeting-a-resistance, which is sound, changes its threshold and its function. In Field 1 the threshold is at the level of physical objects moving against one another: a

48. "When Field 3 is fully realized, there can be no friction between part and part, part and whole—there are no parts, and so no particulars, and no partiality. There is no possible disorientation, for there is only one possible orientation, and that is to be one with the whole" (Burrows, *Sound*, 122).

shoe scraping on pavement, a pen scratching on paper, wind squeezing through a crack in the eaves. Here sound informs us about external events and presences, movements and relationships (and internal as well as when, for example, our stomach gurgles), and orients us as body to our position in and movement against or through the peripheral environment.

In Field 2, where sound takes the shape of language, the force-resistance threshold moves to the demarcation between us and the world, and is specifically localized at the mouth where the forcible movement of breath meets tongue, teeth, and lips in the process of articulating phonemes. Here voice acts as both bridge and barricade in our negotiations with the world, sometimes staking out defensive territorial claims, other times charting regions of shared occupancy, either physical or mental.

In Field 3 sound takes the form of music, voice the form of song. Burrows describes what happens to the center-periphery relationship in Field 3 (we discover center and periphery are a unity) but he does not articulate what happens to the force-resistance dialectic; we must extrapolate what happens to it from his description of the nature of Field 3. In the realm of awareness where center-periphery distinctions collapse in an experience of the unity of the whole, voice, which in Field 2 can be used either as bridge to or as barricade against others, becomes song that is only and always bridge. In Field 3 there are no territorial fights, only celebration of the one common, cosmic space, and the force-resistance dialectic operates at the threshold where the breakthrough against all resistance to what is other occurs. While voice as song is not used to strike out against the other, either in attack or defense, the dialectic of force-resistance inherent in sound remains, however, for it is necessary to the production of the very song that opens up the world of Field 3. What music and song establish, then, is a common threshold where all individual force-resistance dialectics coalesce in a single, shared push against all that keeps humanity resistant to itself, to one another, to the cosmos. In the act of shared singing, all the forces and resistances at play in sound and voice, and in human social interaction, collaborate to generate a transforming unity.

Chapter 3

Liturgical Singing and the Paschal Mystery

COMMUNICATING PRESENCE

Every liturgical rite is structured to facilitate a process of becoming present. Throughout the rite, the ever-present God invites us to become present to the Divine Self and to ourselves as Body of Christ, and to choose a lived presence of surrender to the paschal mystery in daily life.

Sound and voice play a preeminent role in this dynamic of presence. Sound reveals presence, binds hidden interiorities, and manifests here-and-now use of power. When the sound operating is voice, what is revealed is personal presence, personal interiority, and personal power. Voice makes us present to the cultic action because through it we manifest our presence; we declare that we are here and not somewhere else and that we choose to be here. Through voice we reveal otherwise hidden dimensions of our self, both internal physical properties of our body and internal psychic dispositions of our mind and heart. And through voice we commit ourselves from the deepest core, where word originates, to the common purpose of this cultic action.

However, since voice itself makes us present, we must ask why the mere recitation of words is not sufficient to the purpose of liturgy; why is singing required? The answer lies in two actualities of song: the effect of the physical activity of singing on body presence and self-awareness, and the deeper engagement of will and intention involved in the choice to sing.

Singing and self-awareness. Singing activates a deeper vocal resonance than speaking does.[1] Singing begins at the larynx where initial phonation produces vowels rather than consonants. Vowels are more resonant than consonants because they are unstopped sounds that can be prolonged and elaborated by the breath in ways consonants,

---

1. For fuller discussion of this see David Burrows, *Sound, Speech, and Music* (Amherst: University of Massachusetts Press, 1990), 60–65.

the speech-articulating sounds formed by the tongue at teeth and lips, cannot.

Furthermore, singing naturally integrates the body in a kinesthetic sensation of flow generated by the cycle of inhaling and exhaling in connection with phonation. When singing, the body first receives breath, then releases it in a single circular-like movement that flows back upon itself again and again. Although this is also true when we speak, the kinesthetic sensation of the circling of breath, with its sense of continuous flow, is more pronounced when we are singing. Singing generates a sensation of swelling or of expansion of self that, along with the sensation of connectedness with breath (the source of life) and with movement through and with this breath, builds within us a palpable sense of our own presence.[2] As Burrows points out, "The singers themselves have the sensation of expanding, in attenuated form, into surrounding space and filling it."[3] When we sing, we know that we are here, that we are alive, that we are connected, and that we are powerful.

This embodied self-awareness lies at the core of liturgical celebration. Throughout the rite the gathered community encounters God and each other as presence. For liturgy to be this encounter among personal presences, every member must become bodily present and engaged.[4] Singing induces this consciousness because it generates an awareness of physicality that is simultaneously a groundedness in self and a giving of that self away.[5]

Singing as revelation of will and intention. It is by giving voice that we reveal otherwise hidden will and intention. The first level of this self-revelation is the very choice to speak. As David Burrows asserts:

> We cannot choose to have no visual appearance. . . . But we can choose to have no auditory appearance at all simply by remaining

2. Burrows, *Sound*, 98f.

3. Ibid., 20.

4. See Colleen M. Griffith, "Spirituality and the Body" in *Bodies of Worship: Explorations in Theory and Practice*, ed. Bruce T. Morrill (Collegeville, MN: Liturgical Press, 1999), 67–83.

5. For more on the physiology of the relationship between body and sound vibration and its importance for liturgical celebration, see Bruce T. Morrill, with Andrea Goodrich, "Liturgical Music: Bodies Proclaiming and Responding to the Word of God" in *Bodies of Worship: Explorations in Theory and Practice*, ed. Bruce T. Morrill (Collegeville, MN: Liturgical Press, 1999), 157–72.

silent, and this imparts a special quality to the moment we do commit ourselves to speech, or song, or any other sound. The voice . . . is always . . . a manifestation of will and intention.[6]

Because singing originates deeper within the body-self, it reflects a deeper level of self-engagement. The potency of will and intention involved in the act of speech is intensified when we choose to sing. Simply put, more of the self is involved. When we sing we pledge ourselves in a way that is beyond the ordinary.[7] Furthermore, no member of the liturgical assembly can delegate his or her vocal participation to anyone else (be that neighbor, choir, or presider) without loss of personal consent to the action that is taking place.[8]

Liturgical singing is, then, an audible manifestation of presence. By our singing we reveal our personal presence and our disposition to participate with this here-and-now assembled church in the paschal dying and rising of Christ. By our singing we announce that we are here and are choosing to be here in an active, participative, effective way. By our singing we choose to become present to the other members of the assembly. The interiorities we reveal are as unique and variegated as the number of individuals gathered, and it is our singing that puts these limitless variations "into the common pot" of the Body of Christ so that the world may feed from its rich mix.

BECOMING BODY OF CHRIST

Sound not only reveals presence and interiority; it also binds interiorities to one another through the sharing of resonance. Song transforms the sense of self from being separate and isolated to being connected and communal; in fact, this exchange of separation for participation is the ultimate purpose of song. Music enables human beings to discover the essential nature of reality as relationship and to experience their own participation in the fundamental unity-in-diversity that lies at the core of existence. On the level of language and discourse, music crosses over the divides that words alone set up.

6. Burrows, *Sound*, 31.

7. Helmut Hucke, "Musical Requirements of Liturgical Reform" in *The Church Worships*, Concilium, no. 12, ed. Johannes Wagner, and Heinrich Rennings (New York and Glen Rock, NJ: Paulist Press, 1966), 62.

8. Hucke, "Musical Requirements," 59. Perhaps behind the unwillingness of some persons to participate in the singing of the rite is an unconscious awareness of the personal commitment of self that is at stake.

On the level of experience and existence, music dissipates the center-periphery differential between self and other.

Singing crosses over the divisions of language. Voice tied only to language segregates individuals because of its link with semantic reference and the limits these references necessarily place on communication. To say the word "rose," for example, is to make present to imagination what may be physically absent to the senses, and it is through this intangible form of "making present" that persons are brought into closer communication. Yet they remain separated by the fact that there will be as many disparate images of "rose" present in the room as there are participants in the conversation. It may be ontologically true that "a rose is a rose is a rose," but this is never the case noetically.

We remain further separated by the divisions words necessarily establish between speaker and listener. When we engage in conversation, we face off in a way that differentiates us, and, while the feelings and ideas we express through verbalization serve as avenues of connection, we still remain separate and distinct. Because words serve to demarcate these differences, speech has to struggle toward unity by continually spinning new webs aimed at overcoming what the spinning itself separates, divides, and splits.

Music, by contrast, unites us because of its very lack of semantic reference, by what Burrows calls its "protosemiotic" status. Even when tied to words in song, music maintains the upper hand in gaining attention simply because taking it in involves less cognitive effort than does understanding speech.[9] Liturgically speaking, this means that music can focus our attention more quickly than mere speech can. Through music we become present more easily to that speechless realm within one another where the struggle with semantic overload is at rest and the peacefulness of our simple presence can communicate.

Music dissipates the center-periphery differential. Movement through the three fields of human action encompasses a progression from an individualized to a collective sense of self, as the center-periphery relationship of sound shifts from awareness of one's physical body as center in Field 1 to awareness of a shared psychic center in Field 2 to awareness of a central cosmic unity in Field 3. The center-periphery differentiation gradually dissipates and the medium of its dissolution is sound itself as we move from noise (Field 1) to voice (Field 2) to music (Field 3).

9. Burrows, *Sound*, 88.

In Field 1 sound reveals rigid physical boundaries between self as body and the rest of the world. We use sound to discern the relationship between self and nonself in terms of distance. The dog barking down the street is distant; the mail that has just clattered through the slot in our front door is somewhat closer; while the clock ticking at our elbow on the desk is very near. In Field 2 sound as voice/word moves us to a realm of shared consciousness where boundaries become nonphysical and fluid. We open the letter that has arrived and call its sender on the phone to discuss in greater depth the ideas she has written us. The physical distance of even several hundred miles shrinks in the immediacy of shared ideation and feeling that voice allows.

We remain, however, still two separate selves. It is in Field 3, where sound becomes music and song, that the separation between center and periphery is completely overcome. The experience of music—both its production and its reception—induces a sense of collective identity. Immersed in the music's unfolding tensions and releases, harmonizations and rhythms, we face a common horizon. And in the borderless sharing that results, we discover that *we are* that horizon, that the vision, which beckons in front, is the reality planted within, our essential oneness with one another and with all that exists.[10]

Thus it is that singing facilitates our entrance into the cosmic horizon that is Body of Christ enacting the paschal mystery. The unfolding dynamic of presence elicited by the liturgical rite involves a progressive expansion of self-awareness from self-alone to self-in-community to self-in-community-in-Christ.[11] The gathered community undergoes an expansion in sense of identity. And music—above all in its form as communal song—catalyzes the liturgical transformation because it is the shortest, least arduous route across the divide between self and others. Communal singing serves the rite by moving us into Field 3, melting our divisions and melding us into the one embracing circle of the Body of Christ.

10. Dorothy Ling, *The Original Art of Music* (Lanham, MD: The Aspen Institute and University Press of America, 1989) describes this as music's power to move us to "ontological affectivity," a universal regard for and acceptance of others that has nothing to do with individualized comfortability and attraction, but is instead impersonal, gratuitous, and all-inclusive (173).

11. Joyce Ann Zimmerman, CPPS, *Liturgy as Language of Faith: A Liturgical Methodology in the Mode of Paul Ricoeur's Textual Hermeneutics* (Lanham, MD, New York, London: University Press of America, 1988), 183.

Liturgy needs song to catalyze the paschal mystery intentionality at its heart and the presence and communion of the Body of Christ. There is, then, an ontological connection between liturgy and liturgical song in that both open a horizon onto being and identity. Both reveal who we are, music in a generic sense, liturgy in the specific sense of what it means to be baptized in Christ. Music opens the door to a cosmic connection; liturgy specifies the nature of that connection as Body of Christ surrendering to the paschal mystery. This Christian cosmic horizon already exists within the being and identity of the baptized. Liturgical singing facilitates our access to this horizon by being, paradoxically, its centripetal force: by pulling the periphery into the center-self, liturgical singing fractures the limited parameters of the center-self.

LIVING IN LITURGICAL TIME

The concept of time as the separation of past, present, and future is one that facilitates our understanding of physical processes such as the gradual blossoming of flowers in the spring or the eventual corroding of certain metals by exposure to air and water. In this concept the past is terminal and the future inaccessible; they are nonexistent in the present. By contrast, the ritual enactment of originary events reckons time in a different way. In the moment of enactment, time is a ritual *now* that contains within itself all of the past, the present, and the future of the originary, paradigmatic, and eschatological event that is being enacted.

Music is the natural partner of ritual enactment because it is the embodied experience of this reckoning of time. Theology reveals this reckoning through theoretical reasoning; music reveals it through direct experience.[12] Musical meter is not measurement of discrete units, but the continuous flow of an indivisible whole, each present moment

12. Jeremy S. Begbie, *Theology, Music and Time* (Cambridge: Cambridge University Press, 2000) states: "A musical construal of the temporal character of eucharistic repetition can take more adequate account of both Jewish and Christian 'remembrance' (*anamnesis*) and the Eucharist's future anticipation than many eucharistic theologies" (171). See also Robin A. Leaver, "Liturgical Music as Anamnesis" in *Liturgy and Music: Lifetime Learning*, ed. Robin A. Leaver, and Joyce Ann Zimmerman (Collegeville, MN: Liturgical Press, 1998), 405: "[A] one-dimensional, static approach to worship in the present tense needs to be expanded into a three-dimensional experience: of the past we have received, of the present we now share, as we look towards the infinity into

of which both rises out of its past and moves toward its future while containing within itself all its past and all its future. The wave which is meter is time itself acting as a generating force of existence.

Thus in both music and ritual enactment, being and becoming meet in a single moment of *now*, a moment sustained but not stagnant, temporal but not time-bound (in the clock sense), and immediate but far-reaching in both past and future import. Through both cultic enactment and music, we encounter the meaning of *now* through the direct presence of its past and future references. Furthermore, we actively create this presence through engagement in the dialectic of memory (past), attention (present), and expectation (future). Music's role in ritual enactment is to offer us access to this active creation through an immediate, embodied, and sustainable experience of it.

Furthermore, music serves the liturgical role of revealing the force of time as that which makes return also departure. Ricoeur's hermeneutic method shows us how every new liturgical enactment yields new self-understanding and new modes of living. It is the repeated return to our originary event (the paschal mystery enacted in liturgy) that generates our future. We do not return to the past in order to enshrine it, but to be propelled by it into the future. The movement is forward. Yet, in order for this forward momentum to be unleashed, we must return over and over to its originary formulation.

Music bears this same characteristic of infinite return to infinite departure. The dynamic quality of a tone is a "particular kind of unfulfillment"[13] that makes it yearn, so to speak, for what is coming. It finds its completion and its meaning only by moving forward toward cadential resolution. Yet, in a melody as a whole, one resolution often becomes the starting point of a new. Along the journey of a melody as a whole, tones constantly "arrive" and "depart" as one resolution becomes the starting point of a new musical phrase, each arrival a new departure, each completion a fresh start. Music is constantly reaching its goal and departing for its goal,[14] carrying a directional thrust

---

which we are being drawn. Music has a unique power to express and convey all three dimensions simultaneously in our worship."

13. Victor Zuckerkandl, *Sound and Symbol: Music and the External World*, trans. Willard R. Trask (New York: Pantheon Books, 1956; Princeton: Princeton/ Bollingen 1969; 1973), 94; hereafter referred to as *External World*.

14. Zuckerkandl points out that in diatonic music in which tones move away from and back to the fundamental tone, the point of departure and the point of arrival are identical; thus, departing is returning (*External World*, 97).

determined by the parameters of a given diatonic scale, but inexhaustibly free in the manner in which it travels toward this goal.[15] To be "auditively *in* the tone now sounding"[16] is to be caught up in the dynamic tension between its present and its future.[17]

Return becomes departure because of the force of time. Time itself makes ritual return to our originary event an enactment propelling us toward the future rather than a reminiscence or romanticism trapping us in the past. Time does not freeze events and their meaning but frees their generative power. And it is the experience of time in music that moves this understanding of enactment from theological concept to lived experience.[18] Music provides the embodied experience of how the process of transformative self-encounter, which is enactment, takes place through the redemptive power of time. Music shows us that time is not that from which we need to be saved, but that through which, in the all-merciful and incarnational plan of God, we are saved.

This approach differs from that of theorists who view the "return" of sacred time as cyclic rather than progressive. Stephen Plank, for example, follows the lead of Mircea Eliade and separates secular from sacred time.[19] For him, secular time proceeds linearly toward a goal from a goal, while sacred time is the cyclic return of the past in the present. This cyclic return is marked and ushered in by ritual, through

---

"[I]n the tonal field of force . . . *all* paths lead back to their point of departure" (103).

15. Zuckerkandl, *External World*, 99.

16. Ibid., 94 (italics original).

17. Begbie adds that this tension is multilayered because musical meter is multilayered. Resolution of tension on one metric level sharpens tension on other levels, and this amplification works paradoxically to intensify expectation of ultimate fulfillment (*Theology, Music, and Time*, 106–8). With music we learn to enjoy tension because it heightens hope (103). See his ch. 4 for his exposition of how music's multilayered matrix of expectation and fulfillment can expand and clarify our understanding of both hope and eschatology.

18. Zuckerkandl, *Man the Musician*, 350: "[T]he meaning of history is more readily grasped by musical thinking than by logical thinking."

19. Stephen Plank, *"The Way to Heavens Doore": An Introduction to Liturgical Process and Musical Style* (Metuchen, NJ, and London, 1994), 11–19, passim; hereafter referred to as *"The Way to Heavens Doore."* Although he bases his investigation on a different analysis of the liturgical rite and addresses different themes from those pursued in this study, Plank concurs that the relationship between music and liturgy is integral and dynamic.

which "time is lifted up into the timeless."[20] Ritual action formalizes the circularity of time in order that linear, historical time may be consecrated and divinized.[21] The assertions we have made about musical hearing along with the understanding of ritual enactment we have developed suggest, however, that the continual return of the past in the present is also goal-oriented progression toward the future. There are not two tracks of time. Secular linear time and sacred cyclic time are not separate realms whose gap must be bridged through ritual. They are one and the same time, the understanding of which is grasped through musical hearing and liturgical enactment. Where Plank suggests that liturgy invites us to "live *beyond* time,"[22] the work of Zuckerkandl suggests that music invites us to live precisely *in* time. Ultimately this approach suggests that it is *historical* time itself that is redemptive. We do not encounter redemption beyond time but in, through, and because of time.[23]

To return in order to depart is a function of the not yet-already mode of the paschal mystery, a function made present to our consciousness through its musical enactment in liturgical celebration. The dynamic quality of musical tones is identical to the dynamic quality of paschal mystery living. We live the tension between the not yet of soteriology and the already of eschatology. The liturgy ritualizes this tension in the chronological unfolding of its elements. Music's role in liturgical enactment is to help us enter this not yet-already, return-departure nature of Christian living through a sensate, embodied experience of it. Musical temporality shows us how liturgical temporality can be a force bearing on ongoing enactment of Christian identity and mission.

20. Plank, *"The Way to Heavens Doore,"* 29.

21. Ibid., 16.

22. Ibid., 29 (italics added).

23. Begbie approaches the musical implications of time in this same way. His aim is "to show how the experience of music can serve to open up features of a distinctively *theological* account of created temporality, redeemed by God in Jesus Christ, and what it means to live in and with time as redeemed creatures" (*Theology, Music, and Time*, 6–7, italics original). He provides an extended discussion of this point, critiquing the ethos of "timelessness" deliberately embedded in the music of John Tavener as a negation of God's deliberate and redemptive involvement with time in the advent of Christ (144–54).

The choice to become liturgically present, to be the Body of Christ, and to engage in time as enactment of Christian identity and mission is not made without resistance. The intentionality that voice reveals may in fact be at war with whatever or whomever is outside the self. Voice creates community by establishing shared worlds, but voice also fences off private worlds.

Voice is, then, ambivalent. While on the physical level of acoustic vibrations all sound unites disparate bodies, in the case of voice, whether that uniting is for love or ill is determined by the intentionality of the speaker. That intentionality can move in either of two directions—toward the opening of territory or toward its defense, toward sharing space or fencing it. Either direction aims at expanding territory, but the one is solipsistic (claiming and holding territory for self) while the other is interrelational (developing both common space and the number of its inhabitants).

This ambivalence of intentionality is the result of the force-resistance dialectic inherent in sound. Wind whistles only when it meets the resistance of a crack in the eaves; a crystal glass only sings when one rubs a finger against its lip. Likewise, vocalization only occurs when the force of the diaphragm pushes breath against the resistance of the vocal folds in the larynx. Burrows considers this interaction "a symbolic displacement . . . of the interface between self and world."[24] Vocalization expressed in speech, then, manifests two levels of force and resistance—the body's internal pushing of breath through its vocal mechanism and the self's struggle with the confronting world.[25] The operation of power that, as Ong points out, sound always manifests becomes for Burrows more than the physical exertion of energy. Sound as voice is the psychic effort at control and domination.

This force-resistance structure of sound and voice bears many correlations with the soteriological-eschatological dialectic of the paschal mystery. We must note, however, that the two dialectics stand in different theoretical domains. The dialectic of soteriology and eschatology is a theological construct we use to describe the experience of Christian living as one in which the baptized are both already redeemed and not yet fully saved. We further use this construct to define the deep structure of the paschal mystery and then apply it to

24. Burrows, *Sound*, 30.
25. Ibid., 36f.

a structural analysis of liturgical rites as a means of uncovering the rites' deep structure as paschal mystery enactment. The dialectic of force and resistance, on the other hand, is a phenomenological analysis of the origin of sound that Burrows uses as a schema for describing human interaction. He uses the force-resistance phenomenon of sound and voice as a sociological paradigm.

We cannot, then, identify the force-resistance dialectic of sound and voice with the soteriological-eschatological dialectic of the paschal mystery. But we can create analogies. And more important, we can offer correlations indicating that the working out of force and resistance through voice is a substantive enactment of the paschal mystery. Above all other considerations, it is this correlation that makes communal singing an essential and integral part of liturgical celebration.

Analogies: force-resistance as paradigm of the paschal mystery dialectic. As natural phenomena, sound, voice, and music arise from the dialectic confrontation between two opposing energies, one dynamic (force), the other static (resistance). The more intensely the dynamic pole exerts itself, the more intensely must the static pole hold its ground, else the sound fizzles out. We can conceptualize the dialectic of sound and voice, then, as a pushing against-holding ground tension, perhaps illustrated with this image: →←. The soteriological and eschatological poles of the paschal mystery, however, are not physical energies but theoretical descriptions of the Christian condition, one of its struggle and perdurability, tears and work, and the other of its satisfaction and completion, joy and sabbath. Together the two poles generate a dynamic tension that lies at the core of Christian identity and living. This energy is generated at the meeting point of the two poles, that is, at their crossing-over, literally illustrated with this image: ✚. And this is the point at which Christian living becomes a dynamic struggle, the struggle between the force of saving grace and human resistance to that grace. Thus at the heart of "✚" stands "→←."

In Field 3 of human action (the realm of music), we stand at a balance point between the competing forces and resistances of sound, neither clamoring for ascendancy over the other nor crumbling under the other's efforts at dominance. When we engage in communal singing, the very force-resistance of sound becomes the catalyst of our communion (*O mirabilia Dei!*).[26] When we engage in liturgy, we enter

---

26. There is a physical, muscular foundation to this balancing of the force-resistance of sound taught in the Italian *appoggio* approach to breath

Field 3 of human action where we are fully aware of our identity as Body of Christ. The liturgical rite brings the tension of soteriology and eschatology more clearly into focus so that we may surrender ourselves more consciously to the redeeming grace of the paschal mystery. And, to extrapolate from Zuckerkandl, the tones are the medium that makes this happen.

Thus the force-resistance structure of sound and voice provides a paradigm for the soteriological-eschatological tension of the paschal mystery, a model from the phenomenological world of the ontological workings out of Christian identity and mission. What is enacted in the soteriological-eschatological dialectic of the paschal mystery is the force-resistance dialectic of grace and sin, and what reveals how this struggle is playing itself out is our use of voice. Force-resistance as paschal mystery paradigm reveals that union with Christ does not mean absence of tension. Without the rubbing of force against resistance, no music occurs; without the pushing of soteriology against eschatology, no transformation in Christian identity takes place. In the midst of liturgical celebration, resistances toward one another and negative feelings about the demands of paschal mystery living do not disappear; rather, they become God's force of grace (*O mirabilia Dei!*)

Substantive correlations: force-resistance as enactment of the paschal mystery dialectic. In the celebration of liturgy, the force-resistance dialectic of song becomes one of the ways we enact the soteriological-eschatological dialectic of the paschal mystery. The force-resistance plays itself out both within the Body of Christ and between the Body of Christ and the liturgical rite.

Force-Resistance within the Body of Christ

In Field 2 there is an ambiguity about the place of self in the scheme of things. The expansion of peripheral edges through thought and

management in singing. In *English, French, German and Italian Techniques of Singing: A Study in National Tonal Preferences and How They Relate to Functional Efficiency* (Metuchen, NJ: Scarecrow Press, 1977), Richard Miller defines *appoggio* as a balanced interrelationship among the muscles and organs of the torso and neck such that "the function of any one of them is not violated through the exaggerated action of another" (41). During singing the singer experiences a sensation of external muscular motions resisted by internal balancing pressures. The Italian vocal pedagogue Francesco Lamperti calls this balancing of muscular forces and resistances that supports a free and sustainable release of breath the *lutte vocale* or vocal struggle (42).

discourse leaves us standing like a scarecrow in the wind, twisting and turning each time a new idea, new invention, new memory blows across the field of awareness. As the center-periphery boundaries disintegrate, we direct energies toward marking and defending borders. Our desire to share territory meets resistance from our need to control and fence it. In our struggle for security, for finding and holding a center, we use voice to set up barricades against the invasions of others. The center-periphery tension and the force-resistance dialectic of sound actually move at cross-purposes; as the center-periphery tension moves toward dissolution, the force-resistance struggle entrenches energies on both sides of its own internal divide. Thus the two dynamics enter into dialectic tension with each other and, as the power of the one resists/impedes the power of the other, we become resistant to the presence of other selves, other ideas, other uncharted territories.

At the point of entrance into Field 3, however, the center-periphery dynamic totally collapses and the force-resistance dialectic brings its internal tensions into balance. This is the realm of ritual and of music. It is also the moment of "✚." Liturgical singing transforms the assembly's *resistance to* into a *resistance for*. The moment this happens (and this can be a single moment sustained throughout an entire celebration, or it can be an isolated moment needing repeated renewal throughout a celebration) is the moment of the assembly's entrance through their singing into the Field 3 experience of being Body of Christ.[27]

Liturgical singing taps into the deepest level of our being and identity precisely at the point of our most profound choice about who we want to be: at the confrontation with the force-resistance dialectic operating within and among us. Liturgical singing enables us to direct our intentionality toward our identity as Body of Christ by choosing to become present to one another in common awareness of who we are. Our very singing uses our resistance to facilitate our surrender. Liturgical song functions within and among us at the very point where the dialectic of soteriology and eschatology is most phenomenologically present: at the point where we use the force-resistance of

---

27. By the term "moment" I do not mean a discrete clock-determined measurement; "moment" must be understood here in terms of the enacted time of rite and music, a time that, while it has no measurement, has limitless meaning.

sound and voice to express our choice to become present by making ourselves vocally visible, to connect with the Body of Christ by sharing common resonance, and to direct our intentionality toward active participation in enactment of the paschal mystery. In liturgical singing, what happens is conscious surrender of self-centeredness to the other-centeredness of identity as Body of Christ. In liturgy the dialectic of force-resistance plays itself out, never absent (without it there could be no sound, no voice, no song), but in possession of a new level of meaning as the dynamic necessary for genuine surrender of self to the other, which is Christ/Body of Christ.

We run a great risk in allowing music to do this to our natural inclination toward self-defense. Physical survival is closely dependent upon speech.[28] Christ's refusal to speak when on trial for his life, for example, was a telling choice for vulnerability. When we sing, we choose to replace word's powers of defense and domination with music's more vulnerable lack of defensiveness. We give up our shields. Burrows insightfully suggests that "allowing music to win out in [such] a confrontation . . . amounts to succumbing to a mini-death wish."[29] This is precisely the choice liturgical enactment of the paschal mystery calls us to: to put aside personal survival and give up the battle for control.

It is here that we confront the issue of whose voice in the collective arena of the gathered assembly is to be the strongest. Surrendering ourselves to the communal vibration of the Body of Christ requires letting the resonance that leads us through the rite be the voice of Christ. The force-resistance structure of sound reveals that liturgical participation does not mean absence of tension and struggle, and that the balancing of force and resistance in Field 3 can only come about through submission to a single dominant vibration (Burrows calls this a "single, evolving image"[30]). The miracle of singing is that it facilitates this submission and does so without destruction of authentic selfhood and individuality.[31]

28. Burrows, *Sound*, 13.

29. Ibid.

30. Ibid., 68.

31. It must be noted that singing can also impede this process, for even in the midst of communal singing one can hold solipsistic ground. Ling would then call the sounds made, no matter how acoustically attuned, "non-music" (*The Original Art of Music*, 65).

In sound and voice, force and resistance push against one another in a contestation of place: will it be yours, or mine? Only when force and resistance are in perfect balance does the answer become "ours." This balance is achieved when we mutually abandon ourselves, giving up vocal efforts at manipulation and control. Liturgy calls us to consciously relinquish self-centeredness for the other-centeredness of identity with the Body of Christ. The arena of mutual self-abandonment is Field 3 where the soteriology of reactive force-resistance dealings with one another becomes the eschatology of a collaborative force-resistance in the service of our common identity and mission. When we use song to allow this relinquishment to happen, force-resistance takes on new meaning as the dynamic necessary for genuine surrender of self to the Other/other.

Thus singing is normative for liturgy because the very nature of song transforms our willful use of personal power, and does so through a paschal mystery dynamic—the dying-to-self-rising-to-others transmutation of force-resistance wrought by communal song. Through communal liturgical song, we choose to transform our use of power from tool of confrontation to avenue of communion. The ritual balancing of "✚" is enabled by the musical balancing of "→←" used for being *with* others rather than for being *against* them. Both music and rite help us "set aside" the struggle to be in communion with one another by simply allowing us to *be in communion*.

Force-Resistance between the Body of Christ and the Rite

In the course of liturgical celebration, we not only resist one another but we also resist the demands the rite places upon us for presence and participation: "We desire both to be present and to absent ourselves, to communicate and to remain withdrawn. These ambivalences are a normal part of human existence, and we bring them to every liturgical celebration."[32] The force-resistance structure of song reveals that this resistance is essential for the choice of participation to be made. Singing uses resistance to produce itself and this resistance is psychic as well as physical. This means that we participate in liturgical enactment of Christian identity and mission not despite the interior resistances of sinfulness, laziness, self-absorption, reticence, etcetera,

---

32. Kathleen Harmon, "Liturgical Music as Prayer" in *Liturgy and Music: Lifetime Learning*, ed. Robin A. Leaver, and Joyce Ann Zimmerman (Collegeville, MN: Liturgical Press, 1998), 275.

but *because* of them. Communal liturgical singing makes our resistance the foundation of our surrender to the rite. Through singing we are carried along even when we do not want to be, our hearts sing desires hidden to us, and we are made more present to ourselves as we become more present to others. As John Wesley so knowingly directed his congregations: "Sing all. See that you join with the congregation as frequently as you can. Let not a slight degree of weakness or weariness hinder you. If it is a cross to you, take it up, and you will find it a blessing."[33]

A second resistance we experience is to the force of time as force of Christian existence. Becoming truly present to the liturgical celebration and entering its mode of time means allowing time to effect change in us. At issue for the Christian community assembled for liturgy is whether or not we surrender to the force of time as that which shapes the authenticity of our tradition. We carry both a rootedness in the past and a momentum toward the future, and we encounter both in the present liturgical moment of here and now. The natural temptation, however, is to resist the force of time by fleeing the demands of here and now. We Christians do this in both daily living and liturgical ritual, either by preferring a romanticized notion of the past, which resists time's way of introducing the new into Christian discipleship, or by preferring an idealized dream of the future, which keeps us constantly chasing novelty instead of embracing the time-necessitated repetitiveness of both discipleship and ritual.

Essentially what we resist is confrontation with Christian identity as mediated through its ritual enactment and the demands for change this confrontation places upon us. At issue once again is which voice is to be the strongest—that of our personal longing for entrenchment or that of the force of time compelling us to change. Liturgical singing melts this resistance by pulling us physically and communally into time's unitive and generative realm. As we sing, musical time has its way with us, and consciously or not we are pulled into the process of our own transformation.

Thus the force-resistance embedded in communal liturgical singing is a working out of the dying-rising dialectic of the paschal mystery. Communal liturgical singing brings the soteriology of our resistance to dying to self up against the eschatological force of our identity as Body

33. John Wesley, "Directions for Singing, III," in *Select Hymns with Tunes Annext* (London: n.p., 1761).

of Christ. Through liturgical singing we tap into the deepest level of Christian being and identity at precisely the most critical point: at the confrontation between the force of God's call to presence and our resistance to that call, between the force of our identity as Body of Christ and our resistance to unself-centered community, between the force of the grace of transformation and our resistance to change. Communal liturgical singing uses these very resistances to facilitate our surrender to the ritual action. What we do through our singing is enact the dialectic of the paschal mystery through the force-resistance dialectic of sound and voice. What we hear in our singing is the sound of our surrender to the mystery that shapes our very being and life.

By nature, communal liturgical singing catalyzes the personal presence necessary for our full, conscious, and active participation in the rite; it pulls us into the liturgical horizon of our shared identity as Body of Christ; it immerses us in the power of time to change our self-understanding and deepen our commitment to Christian mission; and it embodies in its force-resistance structure the soteriological-eschatological structure of the paschal mystery that is being enacted. Clearly, communal singing is never an accidental accretion to liturgy, but a substantive element that facilitates the dynamism of the rite, participates in its deep paschal mystery structure, and contributes to our transformation into being ever more perfectly who we already are, the Body of Christ.

Chapter 4

Pastoral Implication and Challenges

The singing of the assembly is necessary and integral to liturgy not only because it enhances the festivity of the celebration or illuminates the meaning of a text but most important because it facilitates the assembly's ritual enactment of the paschal mystery. This perspective provides a theological explanation for the role of music that arises from the nature of the liturgy itself. The perspective also offers us an integrating guideline for our musical decision-making. A number of pastoral implications and challenges emerge.

Three parameters—two theological and one methodological—direct our discussion here. First, a paschal mystery foundation and orientation must be central to all our musical decision-making. The most critical question to ask when choosing music for liturgy is: will this particular musical piece, or musical style, or musical approach enable *this* assembly in *this* place to give themselves over to ritual enactment of the paschal mystery? Will this music help them surrender themselves to death so that God may raise them—and the whole human community—to new life?

Second, the primary mode of participation in liturgy must be Body of Christ. In our musical decision-making the critical question to ask is: will this particular musical piece, or musical style, or musical approach enable *this* assembly in *this* place to appropriate their identity as Body of Christ? Will this music lead them to act out of this identity more concretely in daily life? Will this music help them surrender self-centeredness so that God may draw them into the universal embrace of Christ who is all in all?

Third, methodologically we apply the model of the dialectic to some of the musical issues and challenges we discuss. This model formed the backbone of the perspective developed in the preceding chapters where we identified the paschal mystery as a dialectic of soteriology and eschatology and liturgical singing as a dialectic of force and resistance. Here we apply a method rather than actual content, but the method is also its own content, as we shall see. The dialectic approach suggests that opposing poles are not dualistic but holistic; together they constitute one reality and their interplay generates the tension that pushes us toward ongoing self-understanding and transformation. The critical question to ask is: how does the dialectical model integrate what appear to be opposing and mutually exclusive musical concerns, and how, then, does this model open up new insight for us not only about liturgy and music but also about ourselves as Body of Christ?

HELPING THE ASSEMBLY CLAIM THEIR SONG

In their singing, the assembly is doing far more than engaging in a surface structure of the rite (for example, vocalizing a written text or accompanying a procession). Rather, they are actualizing the deep structure of the rite, which is surrender through the force-resistance of song to the soteriological-eschatological dialectic of the paschal mystery. Several implications flow from this statement.

To begin with, communal singing provides all members of the assembly access to their baptismal right and duty to be celebrants of the liturgy. The liturgy unfolds as an action of Christ performed in union with all members of his Mystical Body. Singing lends every voice in the assembly import by releasing into the common acoustic space every person's vibrational resonance, every person's interiority, every person's will and intention, all regardless of voice quality or vocal skill. Moreover, because of the manner in which sound pervades space and binds interiorities, singing is an avenue whereby every member of the assembly gains access to every other member, seen or unseen, near or distant. Only designated individuals perform certain liturgical ministries, such as proclamation of the readings or distribution of Communion, but every member of the assembly carries out the ministry of singing the rite.

To omit singing from a liturgical celebration, then, is to truncate the power of the rite to achieve its purpose. Such an omission cheats the assembly out of the full possibility of becoming who they are meant to be in the rite, the Body of Christ given over for the world. An unsung liturgy contradicts not only the nature of the liturgy, then, but also the identity of the church. Noteworthy here is a development in thinking evident in the 2002 edition of the *General Instruction of the Roman Missal*.[1] *GIRM* 1975 reads: "With due consideration for the culture

1. Hereafter referred to as *GIRM 2002*.

and ability of each congregation, great emphasis should be attached to the use of singing at Mass; but it is not always necessary to sing all the texts that are of themselves meant to be sung" (no. 19). *GIRM* 2002 amends this directive to read: "Although it is not always necessary (e.g., in weekday Masses) to sing all the texts that are of themselves meant to be sung, every care should be taken that singing by the ministers and the people is not absent in celebrations that occur on Sundays and on holy days of obligation" (no. 40). The celebration of Eucharist on Sundays and solemnities is central to our immersion in the mystery of Christ as it unfolds through the liturgical year.[2] *GIRM* 2002 rightfully insists that singing must be a part of these celebrations. Pastorally, we may not always be able to make singing part of a weekday Mass; liturgically, we ought never omit singing from Masses celebrated on the Sundays and the solemnities of the church year. At stake is the right of the assembly to enact their identity as church and to appropriate that identity more fully into daily living.

A second implication here is the pastoral responsibility of selecting music accessible to the particular assembly that has gathered to celebrate. Issues of language and culture must be addressed as well as issues of the particularities that make up the "ethos" of a given liturgical community. This is no easy task, especially considering that the typical parish today is a mixture of many racial, language, and cultural groups.[3]

One of the issues we must struggle with, however, is the very power of music to draw us wherever it will. All of us have at one time or another known the experience of being "carried away" by music. The conundrum of music is that while it is meant to enable the assembly to surrender to the ritual enactment of the rite, music can also readily distract—and even protect—the assembly from the deeper demands

2. Vatican II, *Sacrosanctum Concilium, Acta Apostolicae Sedis* 65 (1964): 97–134; English trans. taken from *Vatican Council II: The Conciliar and Post Conciliar Documents*, ed. Austin Flannery, OP, new rev. ed. (Northport, NY: Costello Publishing Company, 1992), no. 102; hereafter referred to as *SC*.

3. Particularly helpful reading here are Linda J. Clark, and Joanne W. Swenson, "The Altar-Aesthetic as 'Work of the People,'" in Charlotte Kroeker, ed., *Music in Christian Worship* (Collegeville, MN: Liturgical Press, 2005), 112–31; Mary McGann, *A Precious Fountain: Music in the Worship of an African American Catholic Community* (Collegeville, MN: Liturgical Press, 2004); and C. Michael Hawn, *Gather into One: Praying and Singing Globally* (Grand Rapids, MI, and Cambridge, U.K.: William B. Eerdmans Publishing Company, 2003).

of the liturgy. The critical question is whether a given use of music in liturgy pulls assembly members into the deep structure of the rite or in fact pulls them out of the rite by directing their attentions and affections elsewhere. We can be offering the assembly music that is disconnected from the true purpose of the rite. Not all music can support ritual enactment of the paschal mystery. The pastoral challenge is to select music that both honors the deep structure of the rite and effectively engages the assembly in it. This is, in fact, the crucial question that needs to be asked as we move forward with the pressing issues of inculturation and multiculturalism facing today's parishes. What music will enable a given assembly no matter what its mix of races, cultures, nationalities, or languages to engage authentically and efficaciously in ritual enactment of the paschal mystery? Beyond choices about the music itself, how do we lead assemblies to understand the deeper purpose behind the music they sing?[4]

An added challenge is that individuals who are not ready for the demands of the paschal mystery often want the music at liturgy to be entertainment. When those who make decisions about liturgical music yield to this pressure, they betray the music's deepest purpose. For music to facilitate radical and lasting transformation through surrender to the paschal mystery, such decisions must forego superficial solutions that engage people in only a passing way. This means that the decision-makers themselves must be willing to undergo paschal mystery transformation.

The assembly cannot arrive at the celebration of liturgy ready to take on the ritual demands of presence, of collaboration with the Body of Christ, and of engagement in the paschal mystery unless they are already surrendering to these demands in daily Christian living. The pastoral mission of leading the community to authentic engagement in the liturgy is broader than the time frame of the rite itself. The musical task is also broader. Both music and liturgy share a common orientation toward the totality of living. Dorothy Ling describes a musical attitude toward life that parallels the liturgical one. For Ling (and by application, Victor Zuckerkandl) the goal of music-making is to lead

---

4. Addressing this question is the intent of Kroeker's *Music in Christian Worship*; see in particular her Introduction (viii–xvi); her closing chapter, "Choosing Music for Worship" (191–205; and John Witvliet, "The Virtue of Liturgical Discernment" (83–97).

persons to deal with everyday life from a musical frame of mind.[5]
Liturgy aims to lead the Christian community to deal with daily living from the single liturgical attitude of living the paschal mystery.
The baptized need to live every day liturgically; they also need to live
every day "musically." Only then can they come to the liturgy ready
to meet its demands. Critical questions to ask here include: How does
one come to understand liturgy as enactment of the paschal mystery?
How does one come to see Christian living as participation in the
paschal mystery? How does one come to understand the connection
between liturgy and daily Christian living? How does liturgical music
help people see the connection? How can we help assembly members
come to better understand the relationship between liturgical music
and enactment of the paschal mystery?

CHOOSING TO BE BODY OF CHRIST

Because of baptism the paschal mystery of Christ is also our mystery. The paschal mystery carries what we can call an "ontological
vehemence." There is no dichotomy between the mystery of Christ
and the identity of the baptized Christian. Furthermore, while this ontological vehemence marks each one of us individually and personally,
this identity is not a private one but a communal one shared with the
whole community of the church. *We* are the Body of Christ.

Learning to Pray as the Body of Christ[6]

Essential to celebrating identity as Body of Christ is a clear understanding of the nature of liturgical prayer and the role liturgical music
plays in supporting this kind of prayer. In a generic sense, all Christian
prayer engages us in paying attention to the presence of God.[7] God's
presence is free gift. So is our ability to pay attention to that presence
when, amid myriad distractions, blocks and fears, we recognize it.
The divine presence to which we attend may take many forms, from a
constantly felt awareness of God's nearness to the paradoxical sense of

5. Ling, *The Original Art of Music* (Lanham, MD: The Aspen Institute and
University Press of America, 1989), 49.

6. This section is adapted from Kathleen Harmon, "Liturgical Music as
Prayer," in *Liturgy and Music: Lifetime Learning*, ed. Robin A. Leaver and Joyce
Ann Zimmerman (Collegeville, MN: Liturgical Press, 1998), 265–69.

7. James M. Reese, OSFS, "Prayer," in *The New Dictionary of Theology*, ed.
Joseph A. Komonchak, Mary Collins, and Dermot A. Lane (Wilmington, DE:
Michael Glazier, 1987), 790.

God's complete absence. It is not the sense of God's nearness that constitutes prayer, but rather the fidelity of our attention that chooses to trust that, near or distant, God remains God-with-us and God-for-us.

Becoming present to the presence of God means making a conscious choice to do so. There is a difference between being present in a purely spatial way (physically "being there") and being present in a personal sense (psychologically "being with"). We only enter this deeper level of presence when we choose to relate to others with conscious awareness and attention. Prayer requires intentional cultivation of this kind of presence.[8]

Paradoxically, the choice to be personally present to another generates self-awareness and identity, and is a necessary part of healthy personality growth and of Christian development.[9] When physical things that are only spatially present to each other move too close together, they lose their separate identities.[10] Hydrogen and oxygen, for example, become water; blue and yellow become green. In the realm of personal presence, however, authentic union generates greater differentiation. Such union is, in fact, a prerequisite for discovering authentic identity.[11] In making ourselves consciously present to another, we become present to ourselves. Interpersonal communion does not obliterate identity but more clearly delineates it.

For us who are Christian, when this personal presence is to God in prayer, the identity we discover within ourselves is that of Christ. Through the working of the Holy Spirit prayer becomes the fusing of our attentiveness with the attentiveness of Christ. "Christ's own prayer is the privileged prayer that shapes and guides all Christian prayer."[12] The consciousness with which we attend to God becomes

8. J. R. Sheets, "Personal and Liturgical Prayer," *Worship* 47:7 (August–September, 1973): 406–13.

9. See Dietrich von Hildebrand, *Liturgy and Personality*, rev. ed. (Baltimore: Helicon Press, 1960), ch. VII, where he describes progressive degrees of "awakenedness," from a general inclination toward values, to a consciousness of the moral demands made by these values and of one's capacity in freedom to say yes or no to these demands, to a deep inner openness to God and God's presence in one's life. He asserts that this third level is essential for the development of authentic Christian personality.

10. Sheets, "Personal and Liturgical Prayer,"406.

11. Ibid.

12. Peter E. Fink, "Public and Private Moments in Christian Prayer," *Worship* 58:6 (November 1984): 486.

the consciousness of Christ. The story of Israel reveals God as ever present and continually acting to save the people. The revelation given us in Jesus Christ discloses that this God is also *Abba*. As we grow in Christian prayer, then, what characterizes our consciousness is tender regard for *Abba*, and a growing desire to bring all others into *Abba's* salvific embrace.

Because prayer is a conscious act of presence that generates identity, it is deeply personal. Because it turns us outward toward all the other members of the human family, it is innately communal.[13] Its authenticity is evidenced by a growing transformation of attitudes and behaviors in the direction of wider and deeper openness, compassion, forgiveness, and communion. Moreover, what becomes increasingly clear in the course of such prayer is that the way to life can only be found through the path of death. To find ourselves we must surrender in trust to the presence of God in and beyond death. Such is no easy choice, as it was not for Jesus, but Christian prayer is precisely the gradual and ongoing making of this choice. The decision is none other than a growing willingness, on both individual and communal levels, to surrender ourselves with Christ to the reality of the paschal mystery in our lives.[14]

Prayer, then, is conscious attention to the presence of *Abba* who calls us with Christ into the paschal mystery. Prayer is that willing attentiveness whereby we allow our consciousness to be transformed into the consciousness of Christ, a consciousness that awakens both the most deeply personal and intuitively communal aspects of our selfhood.

All Christian prayer flows from and leads to liturgical prayer.[15] Private prayer and liturgical prayer are distinct, but their difference

---

13. Ibid., 492–93: "It is important to grasp that we turn toward each other and outward to all people, not by abandoning the personal journey, but *precisely as part of it*. . . .To divorce either the personal or the communal from the pursuit and discovery of God is to remove them both from the realm of Christian prayer."

14. Sheets, "Personal and Liturgical Prayer," 411: "In the New Testament . . . God's presence is revealed to be a paschal presence. It has come about through the passion, death, and resurrection of Christ. This constitutes a new mode of being present. At the same time, it asks for a new type of response. Paschal presence asks for the reciprocity of paschal response . . . ."

15. David L. Fleming, SJ, "Spiritual Direction and Liturgy," in *New Dictionary of Sacramental Worship*, ed. Peter E. Fink (Collegeville, MN: Liturgical Press, 1990), 1221, points out that even in spiritual direction "there is necessarily

is that of two modalities that stand in dialectic relationship to one another. In general, individual prayer is unstructured, spontaneous, and determined by the existential needs of the person who is praying. Liturgical prayer, on the other hand, is structured, formalized, and determined by preexisting ecclesial patterns. What both have in common is the deeply personal element of attentiveness to the presence of God, and the challenge to paschal mystery living. Where the two forms of prayer differ is in modality: while one is the individual paying attention, the other is the community of the church paying attention. Both modalities are necessary for full surrender to the paschal mystery. Individual prayer engages us in private reflection on how daily living challenges us to live the paschal mystery; liturgical prayer engages us in the public, ecclesial, ritual enactment of that mystery.

This discussion of individual and liturgical prayer points out their mutual elements as well as their dialectic relationship. Both are intensely personal and innately communal. Both are necessary for full Christian living. Yet liturgical prayer holds the primary importance because it stands as the foundation for and completion of all Christian prayer.[16] Liturgical prayer is the primary source of the holiness of the church because of the transformative power of ritual enactment. It is as the body assembled for liturgical prayer that the church most clearly constitutes herself as church and makes her identity and mission tangible to herself and to the world.[17] Liturgical prayer is not collective prayer, as when a group gathers to share individual prayer, but the public, ritualized prayer of the Body of Christ expressing the essentially communal nature of all Christian prayer as shared participation in the mystery of Christ's paschal surrender to *Abba*.

It is in this one prayer of Christ that we, the church, both learn and practice that we do not pass through the paschal mystery alone, either as an isolated experience or for an isolated purpose. Rather, we die and rise precisely in relation to one another: "We are never alone when we embrace the responsibilities of the Paschal Mystery dynamic. We are members of the Body of Christ and share in its collective strength

---

present a prior liturgical setting—the Christian community at worship—in which both parties [i.e., director and directee] are situated and formed. . . . A liturgical spirituality is the foundational spirituality of the church, since it always puts us in contact with some aspect of celebrating the Paschal Mystery which identifies all Christians with Christ."

16. *SC*, nos. 9–10, 14.

17. *SC*, no. 2.

as a mutual embrace."[18] It is the interrelatedness of our individual dying and rising with the dying and rising of all the members of the church that liturgy celebrates. In the public assembly of liturgical prayer we make tangible, to ourselves and to the world, the interpersonal nature of surrender to the paschal mystery.

Because all of liturgy is prayer, the singing integral to liturgy is also prayer. Not just any prayer, however; all liturgical singing must draw the assembly into the modality of liturgical prayer. This means that the first and fundamental task of leadership in liturgical music is not teaching people to sing new songs, but teaching them to pray liturgically. This is a far more difficult and long-term challenge, but it is equally more significant and rewarding. At stake is the ability of the Christian community to understand our baptismal identity and mission and to image this in liturgical celebration. Critical questions here include: How do we discern when the singing of the assembly is in fact liturgical prayer? What formation in liturgical prayer do we need to offer the assembly? What formation in liturgical prayer is needed for the liturgical musician?

Learning to Sing as the Body of Christ

Communal liturgical singing enables conscious surrender to being the Body of Christ enacting, in liturgy and in life, the paschal mystery. Communal singing is, then, perhaps the surest way to prevent liturgical celebration from becoming privatized, because it builds and binds the Body of Christ in ways both conscious and unconscious. Through singing, the sound waves generated by many voices overlap and intertwine, and what enters the body and stirs the soul of each individual is the multivalent vibration of many individuals becoming the one Body of Christ. Through their singing, assembly members make a gift of self to one another that becomes gift of all to God and to the world.[19]

18. Joyce Ann Zimmerman, CPPS, *Liturgy as Living Faith: A Liturgical Spirituality* (Scranton: University of Scranton Press, London and Toronto: Associated University Presses, 1993), 137. See further 137–38: "No one person is the Body of Christ, but together we are members of the one Body with Christ as Head. . . . This suggests that an individual is more than just 'one among many'; an individual holds the Body in the palm of her/his hand by the works s/he performs. Each of us is responsible for the whole Body. Each is co-author of the Christian text, the living document we call 'liturgy.'"

19. Joseph Gelineau, *Voices and Instruments in Christian Worship*, trans. Clifford Howell, SJ (Collegeville, MN: Liturgical Press, 1964), 17, states: "In

To withhold one's voice, then, is to withhold one's self from the assembly. Ironically, however, we can also give voice in such a way that we impede, even defy, the Body of Christ. In her training of musicians for the field of music thanatology (music used to assist persons through the process of dying), Therese Schroeder-Sheker discusses the phenomenon of entrainment in which bodies in a shared acoustic space eventually come to oscillate together at the wave rate of the source giving off the strongest vibration.[20] As illustration of the phenomenon she relates an experiment in which grandfather clocks with pendulums swinging at different rates and times were enclosed in a room; twenty-four hours later all the pendulums were swinging synchronically. This same phenomenon of entrainment occurs whenever human beings engage in the activity of communal singing; individual presences interpenetrate and a single vibrational presence is established and shared. At their own whim, the sound vibrations generated by singing unite the members of the assembly. Yet unlike the grandfather clocks whose action is mechanical and whose response insentient, the assembly members must consciously choose whose voice, whose vibration, will be the dominant one. The dialectic of force-resistance plays itself out as a dialectic between grace and freedom, between Christ as Head and church as his Body, and ultimately, as the

---

singing a man [*sic*] becomes, as it were, a pouring-out and a gift, because song, compounded of the breath which he breathes out from his inmost self and of the sound of his voice which cannot be held or imprisoned, is the free expression of himself, the manifestation of his interior being and the gratuitous giving of his personality. . . . song is the living portrayal of spiritual self-giving."

20. Therese Schroeder-Sheker, "Music for the Dying: A Personal Account of the New Field of Music Thanatology—History, Theories, and Clinical Narratives," in *ADVANCES, The Journal of Mind-Body Health* 9:1 (Winter 1993): 44–45. The phenomenon of entrainment was discovered in 1665 by the Dutch scientist Christian Huygens. Schroeder-Sheker points out that entrainment can be used for good or ill, and that it operates even on the most subtle levels of the electronic sounds that surround us. For more on entrainment and on the effects of sound vibrations on mind and body, see Bruce T. Morrill, with Andrea Goodrich, "Liturgical Music: Bodies Proclaiming and Responding to the Word of God" in *Bodies of Worship: Explorations in Theory and Practice*, ed. Bruce T. Morrill (Collegeville, MN: Liturgical Press, 1999), 165; Jonathan Goldman, *Healing Sounds: The Power of Harmonics* (Shaftsbury, Dorset/Rockport, MA: Element Books, 1992), 14–15; Don Campbell, *The Mozart Effect*, 123.

church carries out the mission appropriated through liturgical enactment, between the Body of Christ and the world.

This leads us to the point that while liturgy needs music, music also needs liturgy. Without the mediating horizon of the Body of Christ, Field 3 of human action,[21] although cosmic, remains only in the realm of subjective phenomenology. There is no guarantee that the horizon music invites the community to enter is that of Body of Christ. Music needs liturgy to specify the nature of the presence, identity, and intentionality being activated. This insight reminds us of the necessity and responsibility to honor all three of the judgments (liturgical, musical, and pastoral) *Sing to the Lord: Music in Divine Worship* indicates are to guide our musical decision-making.[22] The people need to love what we offer them to sing, but that love must be directed first of all toward Christ and toward their desire to become more perfectly the Body of Christ given for the life of the world.

Even when the horizon opened up by the music is Body of Christ, however, there is no guarantee that members of the assembly will use the force-resistance dialectic of song to engage in collaboration with those around them. Liturgical singing only enacts the paschal mystery when the assembly intentionally surrenders through its singing to the liturgy's deep paschal mystery structure. Some (sometimes even all) members will still resist one another. Sometimes (maybe always) every member will still retain some small barrier of resistance to being Body of Christ. The challenge for liturgical music ministers, as well as for pastoral staffs as a whole, is to identify in the parish community what those resistances are (are they racial? cultural? intergenerational? etc.), what is generating them (is it fear? ignorance? lack of spiritual maturity? extreme individualism? etc.) and what ongoing processes and activities can be implemented to help parishioners overcome these resistances.

THE ROLE OF LISTENING AND OF SILENCE

We have talked a great deal about the necessity of voice and song for liturgical enactment of the paschal mystery. But we must also consider the practice of listening and the presence of silence as musical activities that open us to participation in Body of Christ and enable

21. See ch. 2, 56–57.

22. *Sing to the Lord: Music in Divine Worship* (Washington, D.C.: United States Conference of Catholic Bishops, 2007), nos. 126–136.

us to surrender ourselves to the deep paschal mystery structure of the liturgy.

Listening

The activity of singing remains the fullest expression of the assembly's participation in the music of the liturgy. But participation in the music is not limited to singing. Those who cannot sing are not precluded from the fullest participation. The act of listening, whether to the song of the assembly or to the sound of choir or instrument, is an act of musical presence. We are not speaking here, however, of the silence that is a choice to opt out. As I write this, I am thinking of the elderly gentleman in my parish who has asked me to give him every month a list of the music planned for the upcoming Sundays. He cannot read the hymns at Mass because his eyesight is almost gone, so he takes time at home with magnifying equipment to read over the hymns. This way, he says, he knows what the assembly is singing and can join them with his ears and his heart.

How poignantly this senior citizen demonstrates the relationship between hearing and participation in liturgy. From different but overlapping perspectives, Walter Ong and David Burrows[23] both show us how sound and voice make us present. Victor Zuckerkandl shows us how we also become present through hearing.[24] It is musical hearing that reveals to us the real nature of human hearing. In musical listening the ear is a membrane that unites what is outside with what is inside: the two become identical. Musical hearing obliterates the division between inside and outside, subject and object, self and other. Musical hearing opens us to understand true hearing on all levels of discourse. In all the dialogue of the liturgy, in the spoken interactions between presider and assembly, between announcer of the general intercessions and the community praying, between eucharistic minister and communicant, we hear Christ and we become what we hear. In the proclamation of the word and of the eucharistic prayer we hear Christ, the Word spoken at creation and spilled out in the process of our redemption, and we become what we hear. Listening is a requirement for full participation in liturgy, and musical hearing is our training ground.

23. See ch. 2.
24. See ch. 2.

There exists a dialectic relationship between voicing and listening, between sounding and hearing, which embodies the dialectic relationship between the individuals engaging in the communication. Two things go on. One is that there can be no speaker without a listener. There must be differentiation and divided roles. When our listening is musical, however, a second thing happens: the dialectic differentiation between speaker and listener becomes the pathway to interpersonal communion. Listener becomes receiver not just of mere words but of the person of the one speaking. Speaker becomes receiver of the self given through the listener's choice to hear. Even more, in the liturgy both partners become one listening body as they turn together toward Christ who is the unseen source of all that they both hear and have both staked their lives on. The medium is the message, but here speaker and listener together become the one medium—to themselves, to one another, and to the world—of a larger reality: Body of Christ.

Silence

If sound and voice are what reveal presence, what place does silence have in the liturgy? We must begin by realizing that silence is not absence of word, but its expectation,[25] the preparation of our interiority to receive more deeply the interiority of another (although silence can also be merely sleep, or preoccupation, or even deliberate denial of the presence of the other—the issue once again is our intentionality, our willful choice of how to use the personal power revealed through sound and voice). Silence is the source of possibility; without it things on the verge of becoming never have the space or the time they need to be born.[26]

This is the kind of silence we enter, for example, after the presider's "Let us pray" and before his actual praying of the opening Collect at Mass.[27] This is a liturgical silence where we hold a space of silence in the expectation that God will work in that space. We open this silent space jointly, as the Body of Christ. And we open it for God's activity

25. For a thorough discussion of this point, see Bernard P. Dauenhauer, *Silence: The Phenomenon and Its Ontological Significance* (Bloomington: Indiana University Press, 1980); hereafter referred to as *Silence: The Phenomenon*.

26. For fuller discussion of this point, see Kathleen Harmon, "The Silence of Music," in *Liturgical Ministry* 10 (Spring 2001): 93–100; Dauenhauer, *Silence: The Phenomenon*; Max Picard, *The World of Silence*, trans. Stanley Godman, 2nd printing (Chicago: Henry Regnery Company, 1952).

27. *GIRM* 2002, no. 54.

rather than our own. Furthermore, our silence is not directed toward any predetermined outcome; rather, it is meant to open the way for God to act whenever and however God so chooses.[28]

Music itself is filled with silence.[29] There is a silence in music that characterizes all rests but also "all the timeless spaces between the soundings of its successive tones."[30] A truly musical performer is listening to this silence while he or she performs:

> The accomplished performer 'takes his time,' for he [sic] understands that music lives not only by sounds, but also by silences which cause the very soul of the performer or the listener to be steeped in music. The mediocre performer, however, hustles the notes instead of linking them together flexibly and freely: for he fears the breathing spaces and silences which break the continuity of the form when one does not know how to give them their spiritual content.[31]

One of music's functions is to reveal the positive meaning of silence, "to transform a silence when we hear nothing into an *audible nothing*."[32] Music used in liturgical celebration, then, does not replace silence but takes us more deeply into silence. We can mistakenly use the music, however, to avoid the silence. We do this when we conceive of silence as an absence, an emptiness, a void that frightfully reminds us of death. Ironically, the silence does do exactly this. But does not the liturgy itself do the same as it draws us to acknowledge the dying-to-self necessary that God may raise us to new life? Just as death is not the end, neither is silence. Both are the possibility of new being.

Since silence is as much a component of music as is sound, its relationship to liturgical celebration is as integral. In fact, without silence the presence that sound reveals can never be fully acknowledged (hence, why the rite calls for silence after the proclamation of a reading

28. Dauenhauer, *Silence: The Phenomenon*, 18–19.

29. For a fuller discussion of this point, see Harmon, "The Silence of Music," passim.

30. Harmon, "The Silence of Music," 98.

31. Gisèle Brelet, "Music and Silence," in *Reflections on Art: A Source Book of Writings from Artists, Critics, and Philosophers*, ed. Susanne K. Langer (London, Oxford, New York: Oxford University Press, 1968), 116.

32. Victor Zuckerkandl, *Man the Musician: Sound and Symbol*, vol. 2, trans. Norbert Guterman (Princeton: Princeton University Press, 1973; Princeton/Bollingen, 1976), 279.

or the homily[33]). What makes a specific celebration of liturgy non-musical is not the absence of song, but the absence of a breathed rhythm of sound and silence that is truly prayerful. Likewise, what makes a liturgy musical is not the presence of song, but the presence of prayer mediated by a rhythm of sound and silence that is musical. All vocalized sound in the liturgy is inherently musical—the readings, the homily, the singing, the prayers—as is the silence that flows from and toward them. The discerning questions we need to ask are: What is the relationship of silence to ritual enactment of the paschal mystery? What rhythm of sound and silence marks truly musical liturgy? How does the silence of music enter the body (understood both as Body of Christ and as individual body), and what effect does it have? Do we use music in collaboration with liturgical silence or in opposition to it? Do we fill all the silences with sound? Do we choose the liturgical silences or do we merely wait through them for the next sounded moment of music to entertain us?

VIEWING ALL LITURGY AS MUSICAL

Joseph Gelineau once said, "There is no absolute division or contrast between spoken and sung, music and non-music. At a deeper level, there is a unity of the voice in a range of tones and within [a] continuous scale of modes of utterance which covers a wide register of forms and postures."[34] Music in the liturgy encompasses more than song and instrument; it also includes proclamation of texts, recitation of prayers, and many other actions involving words. These words need to be musically rendered, spoken with changes in intonation, and with the rhythms of alliteration and assonance, of phrasing, accent, and meter.

Even more, since the very core of the world is musical,[35] then all the gestures of liturgy are essentially musical. The music inherent in us as human beings is present in all our actions, all our movements, all our voicings of word, and all our moments of silence. The music of the liturgy is found in a rhythm of sound and silence that encompasses the entirety of the ritual from gathering to dismissal, a rhythm natural

33. *GIRM* 2002, no. 45.
34. Gelineau, "The Path of Music," in *Music and the Experience of God*, Concilium, no. 202, ed. David Power, Mary Collins, and Mellonee Burnim (Edinburgh: T & T Clark, 1989), 144.
35. Victor Zuckerkandl, *Sound and Symbol: Music and the External World*, trans. Willard R. Trask (New York: Pantheon Books, 1956; Princeton: Princeton/Bollingen 1969; 1973).

to life and humanity because it resides at the core of being. The musicality brought to liturgy is none other than the musicality of ordinary living.[36] This is the musicality of ordinary listening to one another in conversation, of attending to one another in such a way that we really hear, of moving our bodies in rhythm with the sun and the moon and all the natural environment. Thus joining in the music of liturgy is possible for every human being present in the assembly, even for those who cannot sing. The critical questions we need to address here are: How can we help all members of the assembly see themselves as musical? How can we help them understand that all the moments and all the gestures of the liturgy are musical? How might viewing all the liturgy as musical influence the way music ministers understand and carry out their ministry?

FOR FURTHER CONSIDERATION

In addition to the pastoral challenges and concerns discussed above, there are other issues that would gain from application of the theological perspective that liturgical singing ritually enacts the paschal mystery. What might be gained for understanding the role of music in liturgy, for example, if we applied Paul Ricoeur's textual hermeneutics of participation-distanciation-appropriation to the music itself? On a generic level, we can use the work of Zuckerkandl to say that every act of music-making is a moment of distanciation that brackets participation in being, elicits new self-understanding, and offers new possibilities for human living. On a specific level, we could investigate the functions of particular musical elements in the rite. For example, is the responsorial psalm a particular moment of distanciation that allows reflection on what the proclaimed word presents for Christian self-understanding, and is the gospel acclamation a moment of appropriation when the assembly chooses Christ as their Ideal?

Second, we might investigate to what extent music itself is an enactment of being and identity, and how this intensifies its facilitation of the ritual enactment of being and identity which is liturgy. One can extrapolate from Zuckerkandl that music-making parallels the nature of liturgical enactment. Both music and liturgical enactment arise from participation in being, and both enable the self-awareness that recognizes identity as fundamental participation in that being. Music is the medium that enables the enactment of identity as oneness with

36. See Ling, *The Original Art of Music*, 48–49.

the world (Burrows would agree); liturgy is the medium that enables enactment of identity as Body of Christ. Both identities are essentially related, for the unity-in-diversity that is Body of Christ is a theological specification of the unity-in-diversity that is the cosmos.

Third, more needs to be said about the nature of time as a force of existence and what light this notion can shed on understanding the role of time in ritual enactment and the liturgical year. If, as we have maintained in this book, time is a determining factor in the ongoing transformation of Christian identity and mission, and not just a passive bystander or accidental conduit, what does this mean for the Christian community's involvement in history, both in its day-to-day unfolding and in its grand sweep? How do liturgy and liturgical music pull the Christian community into time as transformation? How do they make the community both comfortable in the world of human events and committed to actively transforming these events for the sake of Christ?

Fourth, the functionality of liturgical music needs to be examined both in terms of the structural dialectic of the paschal mystery and the unfolding dynamic of presence. For example, what does the entrance song do in terms of the dynamic of presence? What do the eucharistic acclamations do? In terms of the structural dialectic, does the responsorial psalm carry the same soteriological import as the Liturgy of the Word in which it occurs? How does it draw the assembly to the Ideal Presence of Christ proclaimed in the gospel, and what does this mean for its performance?

Finally, more study needs to be done concerning the physiological effect of sound vibrations on the body, specifically in relation to liturgical celebration. Are there forms of music whose intervallic structure and harmonic overtones would move the assembly more quickly to intentional presence and communal identity? Are there instruments that do the same? Are these forms and instruments universal, or do they vary from culture to culture?

Conclusion

In the introduction to this book I cited Aidan Kavanaugh's assertion that "[m]usic is the mode . . . by which the liturgical act gets done" and raised two questions generated by this dictum: what is the liturgical act that is being done, and why is music the mode of its doing? To the first question I have answered that the liturgical act being done is ritual enactment of the paschal mystery. To the second I have answered that communal singing is integral and necessary to liturgy because by its very nature this singing facilitates the gathered community's ritual enactment of the paschal mystery. I have concluded my investigation by applying this theological perspective to some issues and challenges pastoral musicians face, demonstrating the fruit that can result from consistent application of an integrating theological vision.

I hope the theological vision that communal singing is integral and necessary to liturgy because it facilitates and participates in ritual enactment of the paschal mystery will provide those engaged in liturgical music a theological grounding for their ministry. I hope the lens of the paschal mystery will help them make better sense of what they do, giving them an interpretive tool that sheds light not only on their doing of music but also on the living of their daily lives. At its core, our liturgical singing enables us to enter the most radical level of our identity and mission: to be the Body of Christ dying and rising for the sake of the world. May we sing with full awareness, joyful intention, and gladsome surrender.

Index